THE ESSENTIAL GUIDE TO CHARLOTTE REAL ESTATE

INSIGHTS FROM FOURTEEN LOCAL EXPERTS

ANNA GRANGER
ANDY REYNOLDS
SAM GROGAN
AMBER GARCHAR
CHRIS BONNEFOUX
BRAD ROCHE
LISA ARCHER
DARIN BROCKELBANK
LINDA BEVERLEY
LESLIE J. DALE
KIM YORK
DICK YORK
BRENDA THOMPSON
MIKE WAITE

Table of Contents

Introduction

For many years Charlotte, North Carolina has been among the top five fastest-growing major cities in the United States. The estimated population according to the U.S. Census Bureau was 810,000 as of 2014, making Charlotte the 17th largest city in the United States and second largest in the Southeast, based on population. The Charlotte metropolitan area had a 2014 population of approximately 2.4 million.

The Charlotte region's growth has been stimulated by a great business climate, attracting many Fortune 500 Company Headquarters and other major business operations to the area. It is the second largest banking center in the United States after New York City.

Charlotte has a true four-season climate, without extremely cold or hot weather. It is midway between the mountains and the beach and the area has an abundance of recreational opportunities for everyone. Sports fans have a lot to choose from including the NFL Carolina Panthers, the NBA Charlotte Hornets, major NASCAR races, PGA golf championships and major college sports.

With all of the growth comes a large demand for land, construction, real estate development and sales, financing and associated activities. The Charlotte area traditionally had much undeveloped land with little natural boundary constraints, which has allowed for growth in all directions, from the Center City, outward.

In this book, we have brought together fourteen award-winning local leaders in real estate and associated industries to give an overview of the Charlotte real estate market and to provide advice on buying, selling, financing, improving and investing in residential properties in the area.

Anna Granger discusses buying and selling real estate in the South Charlotte area, a large, popular area with lots of shopping and a wide variety of residential neighborhoods. Andy Reynolds covers the Lake Wylie area, a large recreational lake with many residential neighborhoods, just adjacent to Charlotte on the Southwest boundary and along the border with South Carolina. Sam Grogan provides advice on buying and selling luxury properties in the Charlotte region, from Uptown/Center City to the lakes and to the luxury developments in the southern sections of the city. Amber Garchar discusses buying and selling real estate at Lake Norman, the largest man-made lake in North Carolina, and the surrounding towns, just North of Charlotte.

Chris Bonnefoux covers Uptown Charlotte, with dozens of high-rise condominium buildings, all within walking distance of the 100,000 jobs and numerous sports and entertainment venues and restaurants in Center City. Brad Roche discusses residential property financing and shows how to save money when purchasing or refinancing a property. Lisa Archer provides advice on selling and buying homes throughout the greater Charlotte region, along with some programs to help local heroes. Darin Brockelbank discusses improving your property with outdoor living spaces and offers advice on selecting a reliable contractor to handle the construction and maintenance.

Linda Beverley and Leslie J. Dale cover investing in residential real estate in the Charlotte area and offer advice to new investors as well as to investors new to the area. Kim and Dick York discuss buying and selling real estate in the rapid growing Greater Northeast Charlotte area, that includes the UNCC area and parts of both Mecklenburg and Cabarrus Counties. Brenda Thompson provides advice on buying and selling unique properties in the Western North Carolina Mountains, about two hours to the West of Charlotte. Mike Waite offers advice on how to select a residential remodeling contractor, reducing both your risk and your stress.

Royalties from sales of this book are being donated to The Humane Society of Charlotte. Since 1978 the Humane Society of Charlotte has been a community resource committed to improving the lives of companion animals through adoption, spay/neuter and education. The vision of The Humane Society is for all companion animals to one day live in a community full of care and compassion without the fear of being unwanted.

Chapter 1

Anna Granger

South Charlotte Real Estate

I have been helping buyers and sellers with their residential property transactions in the Charlotte area since founding my agency, 1st Choice Properties, in 2004. I help buyers and sellers throughout the greater Charlotte area with a wide range of property values, generally anywhere from the mid $100,000s to over a million dollars. Before founding my agency, I was a real estate investor for a few years and decided that my enjoyment working with people to help them achieve their goals would fit well with being an agent. I decided that I wanted to own my own agency from the start, as that would allow me to provide the highest level of individualized service to every buyer and seller. We are a small firm, but that gives us much more flexibility and we don't hesitate to spend quite a bit on extra marketing that will benefit our sellers.

Selling Your South Charlotte Property

I really enjoy helping people understand what it takes to sell a home and working with sellers as a team to get their goals accomplished. I always tell my clients the marketing of the property starts way before it goes on the Multiple Listing Service (MLS) and before the sign is in the yard. It starts the day we work together and we plan and strategize how to price the house, what we should change, what should be added, things like that. If you do the right thing from the very beginning, there is less stress and selling the house is much faster. My formula seems to be working as my average listings stay on the market for only about half of the area average.

Sellers always want to know the price their house is likely to sell for. Agents will do a competitive market analysis, but make sure that the agent substantiates the expected pricing and shows the analysis behind the pricing estimate. The most critical factor in properly marketing a property is having the correct price, not underpricing, nor overpricing a property. Some may think that overpricing is a good strategy, but that mostly leads to lack of buyer interest. When working with a prospective seller I look at the competition, absorption rates, demand, supply, and I also go out into the neighborhood and look at the competition by previewing other active listings that are in competition with the seller's home. It is important for the seller to receive honest feedback on the condition of the property and the other factors that will determine how well the property will sell.

Once a decision is made to list a home, it is now a product, and the agent and owner need to make the product as attractive to as many people as possible. It is time to emotionally detach from the home. Now it is time to market a property, not a home. When selecting an agent make sure the agent describes the marketing program that will be used. All agents will get the property listed in the MLS, so all agents provide that basic measure of exposure. The real differences show up in the different approaches to marketing the property, how creative the agent is in marketing the property and how much the agent will spend on the marketing campaign.

Work as a team with the agent to identify what needs to be done to get the house in condition to be viewed. It takes work to get a home show-ready, but it never fails. It can take between two to four weeks depending on the condition of the property, what needs to be done and the individual situation of the seller. Although it is very rare, sometimes people live in showcase homes that are almost ready to show. One of the most important actions is to de-clutter; renting a storage unit is a practical solution to removing excess clutter. Sometimes I will hire a stager to help or to bring in some furniture. Small investments, like touching up the paint or painting where needed, make the house look fresh and can pay off in a better sales price and will help the house sell faster. Make sure the front of the property and front yard are in good condition so there is "curb appeal". The seller only gets one chance when a prospective buyer comes in the door and it makes a huge difference. A lot depends on the situation of the seller and what budget the seller has available. The agent needs to understand that every client is unique and what works for one may not work for another.

What Sellers Are Saying:

"One of our best decisions! Anna was amazing! This was my first experience selling a home. We interviewed many relators, but Anna was special. I wanted someone who would work as hard as I do, provide expertise and support us as we moved through the process. Anna was everything I could have asked for and more. She is special in that she respects her clients, and happy to provide advice (which I asked for a lot). Anna also understands and respects her clients opinions and choices. Anna makes you feel like you are her only client. She was always available and willingly spent whatever time we needed speaking with us. Most important to me was Anna's support. She was with us every step of the way, providing advice and often times just helping me and my husband to stay calm when challenging situations arose. We had a situation where we needed repairs done and were being quoted many thousands to have them done. Anna worked with us to find reputable contractors, gather opinions, and decide on the best course of action. We ended up only needing to spend a few hundred dollars as opposed to the many thousands we were originally quoted. In the end we got the price we asked for, only had our house on the market a couple days, and only needed to spend a reasonable fee for repair work. If you are looking to sell a home, Anna Granger is the best!"

- Jen V.

"We had to move due to a relocation and Anna could not have been more helpful. This was our first time selling a home; I wish we had her when we bought the home. She provided fantastic advice on what to update, what to worry about and what to really expect from the market. She has a network of painters, cleaners and others to help with anything you might need. We asked thousands of questions and never, ever felt like we were a burden. There were plenty of text messages back and forth as well. Anna was always available and easy to get in touch with. Anna helped secure the best price for our home and we couldn't have been more satisfied with her efforts along the way. Bottom line, you should work with Anna."

-Sarah W.

Buying Your South Charlotte Property

Buying a home is likely the largest investment a family will make so it is important to consider the time frame for expected ownership. In recent years it is not likely to be a profitable investment if the ownership timeframe is only a year or so. Sometimes, buyers can get emotionally attached to a property they view and not consider if it is really a good long-tern investment. I recommend that buyers consider if it will be what they want for at least three to five years and also to think about resale potential later. If there are certain features that the buyer doesn't like, consider if that could also hinder a resale to a future buyer.

Many potential buyers will work with a mortgage company to get preapproved for financing. This is a good practice as it signals to sellers that you are a qualified buyer and it removes some of their risk. Often the buyers get preapproved for a higher amount than they really intend to spend and may then start thinking about purchasing a more expensive house. My advice is to not overspend just because you have been preapproved for a higher amount, especially young families just starting out. Consider the financial risk of larger mortgage payments than had originally been planned. I really enjoy helping people make good long-term decisions when it comes to purchasing a home.

The South Charlotte area and into the adjoining part of Union County has a very diverse range of residential neighborhoods, from the highly developed metro neighborhoods to mostly suburban areas. There are even opportunities to live in developments within the Charlotte city limit that have a rural character with large lots. Along with price range, one of the first considerations is the character of the neighborhood the buyer is interested in making their home. Other important considerations would include quality of schools serving the area, distance to schools and work, amenities such as parks and clubs and commuting traffic considerations.

Condition of resale properties is always a concern for homebuyers. Information on property condition starts with the property disclosure statement that is part of the listing. The disclosure provides the age of the roof and major systems such the water heater and HVAC system as well as other known issues at the property. I help buyers assess the potential replacement costs based on the age of the systems. Buyers should take into consideration the additional investment that may be required to replace major systems not long after the property purchase if the systems are near the end of their useful lives.

There are some other possible conditions relating to the property that should be evaluated during the decision-making process. Some of the most typical additional factors are if the property is subject to a Home Owners Association (HOA); Covenants, Conditions & Restrictions (CC&Rs); access by a private road; if the property is in proximity to a flood zone; or the property is served by a septic tank.

13

If the property is in a development that is associated with a Home Owners Association (HOA), it is important to review the terms of the HOA. There will be a membership cost involved that can be a small amount or it might be a significant amount depending on the level of maintenance and upkeep that is provided by the HOA. CC&Rs, and many times HOAs, place restrictions on what can be done with the property, so it is critical to review any such restrictions. These could include restrictions on modifications or expansions, the type of fencing allowed and even restrictions on plantings used in the lawn and yard. Ultimately this could be an important factor if the CC&Rs or the HOA regulations restrict the buyer's intended future use of the property.

Properties with access by a private road will have a requirement that homeowners served by the private road pay for the maintenance and repair. There will be periodic maintenance charges and the potential for a large expense if a major repair is needed. There are a lot of creeks in the Charlotte area, so I help prospective buyers assess the proximity of the property to flood zones. I work with NCFloodmaps.com and insurance agents to determine if the property is in, or near, a flood zone and what the implications for insurance cost may be.

Much of unincorporated Mecklenburg County and Union County do not have city services, so in such cases the properties have septic tanks. Charlotte's city limit has rapidly expanded through annexation to the south and southeast over the past several years, so even within the city limits, many neighborhoods built before incorporation have septic tanks, even if city sewer service is currently available. An important consideration is if the septic tank is properly sized for the amount of bedrooms currently in the house. There are cases where current or past homeowners have converted rooms into bedrooms and the septic tank may not be adequate for the current configuration and a large expense could be required to make the property conform. This could also limit possible expansion of the house.

After selecting a property and coming to an agreement with the seller, it is time for some final due diligence. I always recommend that buyers contract for a property inspection with a qualified inspector and a survey. In addition to structural and systems inspections, buyers should have a termite inspection and radon test. The inspector often finds structural or system issues with the property that may not be known to the current homeowners. If the property has a well, a water test is recommended, and if the property has a septic system, a septic inspection should be conducted. The inspections and tests can add up to more out-of-pocket expenses for the buyer, but there is peace-of-mind in knowing that expensive systems are in proper condition. Findings of substantial issues with the property can result in a negotiation with the seller to remedy or to take the cost of remediation into consideration in the purchase price. Most surveys do not result in findings of issues; however, there are cases where the survey uncovered something that no one knew about. For instance, a landfill area was found by a surveyor on a property with the result of cancelling a transaction. If something like this were not discovered, it could be an issue years later, when the buyers are trying to sell.

A final important piece of advice for buyers is to work with an agent that has many years of experience in the specific area where you are interested in purchasing. A well-experienced agent that is an expert on the area will know what to look for when it comes to conditions that might not be apparent to someone new to the area, such as sources of noise, pollution, traffic or planned new roads or highways in the area. Make sure the agent is really an advocate for you and keeps your long-term interest in mind, not an agent just looking to receive the highest commission

What Buyers Are Saying:

"We have bought and sold several properties and have worked with good realtors every time, but Anna Granger is clearly THE best there is anywhere! From our first phone call to her inquiring about a property, right up until our closing, she has been 100% supportive of us and totally prompt. We asked to see a certain home and within a few hours she had us in the house to view it. The next day we asked to see the house again, and sure enough, no problem! When we decided to bid on the home, Anna was helpful in the process in guiding us to make an appropriate bid. Once we had the sale pending, she arranged every detail for us, from suggesting surveyors, bug inspectors, home inspectors, attorneys, and even a general contractor for some needed repairs. We used each of her suggestions and were very pleased with all of the people whom she suggested. If we had a question about any part of the process (and we had many), a simple text or email to Anna produced an almost instant response from her. She was at closing with us and was simply a great support system as well as advisor in this entire process. We can't say enough good things about Anna and will definitely use her for any future real estate transactions that we may encounter. She is simply superior in every way."

-Mary Beth B.

"Anna did a great job working with me to find a home in the area that I wanted. She was available and responsive at all times and helpful not only in finding a home, but throughout the purchase process. She worked to provide all contractors, due diligence personnel, and my bank with any information that was needed to complete the sale in a timely manner. As a first time homebuyer, I was reliant on much of her skill, expertise, and advice during the process. I was very happy and would recommend her to anyone looking to purchase a new home."

-Matt D.

Featured South Charlotte Neighborhoods and Areas

Providence Plantation
Providence Plantation is a large subdivision with a feeling of country living within the city. Much of Providence Plantation was developed with large (acre plus) lots and the neighborhood is heavily wooded. The Arboretum and other shopping centers are nearby and there is a racquet and swim club in the center of the development. Home values generally range from $300,000 to $800,000 and there are some homes valued over $1 million.

Hembstead
Hembstead is a suburban neighborhood near the Arboretum Shopping Center, close to the intersection of Highways 16 and 51. Although it is close to shopping and restaurants, it has a sense of privacy. The lots tend to be larger than average on the tree-lined streets. The neighborhood includes nature paths and there is a private swim and racquet club available to homeowners. Home values in the neighborhood typically range from $400,000 to $800,000.

Providence Country Club
Providence Country Club is at the southern limit of the City of Charlotte along Providence Road. The neighborhood surrounds the beautiful private golf course designed by Dan Maples and most homes have a golf course view. The private club also includes a Georgian design clubhouse and tennis courts and swimming pool. Home values in the neighborhood range from $450,000 to over $1 million.

SouthPark
The SouthPark area is the shopping, restaurant and business hub of the South Charlotte area. Located about six miles from Uptown Charlotte, SouthPark area businesses employ over 40,000 people. Living in SouthPark means close proximity to one of the largest and most exclusive malls in the country as well as dozens of fine restaurants. There are a variety of neighborhoods in the SouthPark area, from

townhome communities and older neighborhoods with smaller single-family homes to gated luxury communities. Home values typically range from $350,000 to over $1 million and to several Million dollars in the luxury communities.

Ballantyne
The Ballantyne area along Charlotte's border with South Carolina is the largest planned community in Charlotte. Along with a variety of housing, it is home to a large corporate office park and several shopping centers. There is a wide variety of housing in the area from apartments and townhome communities, many individual neighborhoods with single-family homes, to the exclusive Ballantyne Country Club community. Home values start around $250,000 and are up to several million dollars at the country club.

Raintree
Raintree is a large planned development with seven distinct neighborhoods built around the 36-hole Raintree Country Club. Raintree has a natural rustic setting yet is close to the Arboretum and near other shopping and dining areas. Most of the homes within Raintree have a golf course view. Homes in the area range from townhomes with values starting around $150,000 to single-family homes valued up to $500,000.

Beverly Crest
Beverly Crest is a planned development of seven individual neighborhoods near the intersection of Providence Road and Highway 51. It is near the Arboretum shopping center and Providence High School. The Beverly Crest Swim and Racquet Club amenities are available to residents of the development. The community offers both townhomes as well as single-family houses. Values range from $230,000 to $500,000.

Lansdowne

Lansdowne is a large neighborhood of mostly modern style houses built in the 1960's that stretches from Providence Road on one side all the way to Sardis Road. It is a very convenient location in the middle of South Charlotte, only minutes from both SouthPark Mall and Cotswold Mall and short drive to Uptown Charlotte. Homes in the neighborhood range from $230,000 to $450,000.

Town Of Matthews

The Town of Matthews borders Charlotte along the southeast edge. Matthews has a picturesque, historic downtown but most of the town has a modern suburban character. The town is growing rapidly, with both residential and commercial development along major thoroughfares. Matthews has a variety of neighborhoods from townhome communities to luxury developments. No matter where the location in Matthews, shopping is nearby.

Town of Mint Hill

The Town of Mint Hill is a suburban town that borders both Matthews and the southeast edge of Charlotte. Mint Hill has a small town character with substantial undeveloped land, although there has been significant residential and commercial development in recent years. There are a variety of neighborhoods in Mint Hill ranging from townhouse communities up to luxury equestrian and golf estates.

About Anna Granger

Anna Granger is the owner and broker-in-charge of 1st Choice Properties Inc. in Charlotte, NC. She created the agency in 2004 and represents buyers and sellers throughout the Charlotte area. She is a licensed broker in both North Carolina and South Carolina. Anna has an MBA and has earned a number of real estate industry designations. These include SPS (Strategic Pricing Specialist), ABR (Accredited Buyer Representative), SFR (Short Sales and Foreclosure Resource) and ePro (Internet Professionals).

Anna has been voted a Five Star Real Estate Agent in Client Satisfaction for seven consecutive years, from 2009 through 2015 by Charlotte Magazine. In addition to English, she speaks fluent German and helps a number of international buyers and sellers with property transactions in the Charlotte area.

1st Choice Properties Inc. is a small firm (four agents at the time of publication) and is dedicated to providing personalized attention to every client. The firm helps both traditional buyers and sellers with home transactions and also helps investors locate and purchase single-family residential investment properties. The firm also helps with land deals, short sales and foreclosure transactions.

For more information about Anna Granger and 1st Choice Properties, visit,
http://www.1stChoiceProperties.us.

Chapter 2

Andy Reynolds

Lake Wylie Area Real Estate

Having grown up in the Lake Wylie area, I have always enjoyed the small-town charm and enriching lakeside activities, such as boating and waterskiing on the lake. I also worked in boat sales here on Lake Wylie before I became a Realtor. My lifelong experiences on the lake have made me very familiar with the needs of clients moving into and out of the area. With a license in both North and South Carolina, I help buyers and sellers within roughly a twenty-mile range around the lake.

The homes near Lake Wylie tend to start around $300,000 and many go up to over a million dollars on the waterfront. I enjoy helping buyers and sellers in the entire range of property values and also love working with first time homebuyers off the lake, below that range. Their excitement and energy gives me that emotional high that got me into this business in the first place. I also work with custom-home builders and also with people who are interested in raw land on the waterfront where they can build their dream home. My personal philosophy is simply to treat people the way you want to be treated. If you do that everything will work out.

Selling Your Lake Wylie Area Property

Working with people to sell their properties for the highest price so that they can move on happily is one of the best things about my work. With waterfront property, there are a lot of variables, so we really want to make sure that sellers have a solid understanding of their property's worth and the right approach to marketing it before we begin. With waterfront property, in particular, there are many factors that influence the value that all have to be taken into account. Knowing what prospective buyers will be able to do with the land or the existing house, and what they won't be able to do, will help put a correct price on the property. Lakeside sellers should work with a waterfront property expert so they can come up with a value that truly represents the worth of their home. It really isn't the same as selling in a subdivision of similar properties, where the house can be valued according to a specific average price per square foot.

The lake view from the property is a very large factor in property valuation and can change the property value by as much as $300,000. There's a big difference between a wide-sweeping view on the open channel to a narrower but more secluded view in a cove. The length of shoreline and water depth at the property are also important factors. Water depth will affect the ability to dock a boat at the property. Regulations at specific locations can also affect the ability to construct a dock or to expand a dock. There are also restrictions on how close to the water a structure can be constructed, and be aware that some existing structures at the lake do not conform to current restrictions. Lack of adequate distance between a house and the lake can prevent a buyer from expansion or construction of a pool.

It is important to take into account the composition of the lake along the property. Some parts of Lake Wylie are filling in with sediment. Some parts get very muddy during the rainy season because lots of streams and creeks empty into the lake, whereas other parts of the lake remain clearer even during inclement weather. The slope of the property is a consideration, as well, for some buyers. As an example, retirees tend to want a flatter property, allowing easy access from their home to the boat dock and lake.

Properly marketing a property is critical to get it exposed, not only to the highest number of buyers, but also to the most qualified buyers. Make sure to have your agent describe the marketing program that will be implemented to properly expose the property. Our waterfront properties tend to have higher prices and need to be marketed to luxury homebuyers, and not just in the local area. Many of our buyers are relocating, so it is important to make sure the property will be advertised not only locally, but also on a range of online sites. A property should be showcased with professional photos and possibly a video so that online viewers can get a good feel for the property, without even being physically present. Today, we will even use aerial drones for outdoor videos of larger properties.

A common misconception is that sellers should price a house higher than the real value and wait for an offer to start negotiations. This is not a good strategy. Instead of the expected result, what more typically happens is that there are no offers attracted at all, so there are no negotiations. The listing then goes stale and the seller loses any chance to make an impression. It is important to price the house at the realistic market value and to wow potential buyers right at the outset.

Make sure that any needed repairs are completed and that the home is in proper condition for showing and selling. First impressions are important and make sure your agent is working with you to evaluate how to properly stage the house. This will involve removing any clutter, but it also could mean removing some large furniture, countertop appliances and some personal effects. Buyers will also want to view storage space so make sure closets, kitchen cabinets, garage, attic and basement are all organized and will not detract from the viewing experience.

Many people are already sitting on the fence about whether or not they should buy, so they want to walk into a clean, updated, quality home without a lot of needed work, and they want it to be priced correctly for the market. As a seller, if you can meet these conditions, chances are you'll sell your house quickly.

There are several considerations for selecting an agent for selling your Lake Wylie area property. Proper pricing is critical for a timely sale so make sure your agent has substantial experience representing Lake Wylie area buyers and sellers and can provide good reasoning for the suggested pricing. As mentioned earlier, waterfront property has many more pricing variables, so make sure the agent can demonstrate a large quantity of successful closings on waterfront properties represented. Past client reviews and testimonials will additionally provide an indicator of agent success and working relations with clients.

What Sellers Are Saying:

"Andy Reynolds worked hard for us and sold our lake home on Lake Wylie. He was always responsive and professional even though he has a laid back demeanor. He is easy to talk to and not pushy in the least. As a lifetime Lake Wylie resident, he has significant area knowledge and gives good advice based on his experience and market conditions. His insight proved spot on. I have worked with numerous Realtors over the years and Andy is by far the best I have experienced. I cannot recommend him highly enough".

-Mike M.

"It is a pleasure to write and rate Andy Reynolds, for he is truly one of the finest agents that I have ever met. He is honest, he is knowledgeable, he is professional, he knows his market and uses the latest tools in his quest to be the area's finest agent. We have our personal home listed with Andy and being one of the area's largest homes, we did not make the selection of an agent lightly. It is a pleasure to recommend Andy and his personal services to all seeking to buy or sell their home, commercial or investment property."

-Jim W.

Buying Your Lake Wylie Area Property

The same considerations relating to value discussed for sellers hold true for buyers as well. As a start, lake area buyers need to ask themselves what they really want in a home and to consider the budget for the purchase. I recommend that buyers be pre-qualified or pre-approved for financing, as that will provide an important indicator for the maximum price that can be afforded. In today's market, sellers prefer a pre-approved or at least a per-qualified buyer to minimize the chances of unexpected obstacles that will keep a buyer from closing on the purchase.

With 325 miles of shoreline, Lake Wylie has many neighborhoods, each with its own character. Buyers need to consider the type of neighborhood they would be interested in for their home. Availability or proximity to amenities such as the shoreline, boating, golf, tennis or swimming pools should be considered. We are in close proximity to Charlotte and the airport, but maximum commute time will also be an important consideration. The lake is on the border between North Carolina and South Carolina and several counties are around the lake, with different school systems, so the character of the school system will also be a consideration for families with children.

If interested in lakefront property, view (on an open channel or more secluded in a cove) and water depth for access for a boat are major property value influences. Another important consideration for a lakefront buyer is a dock for a boat or the ability to construct a suitable dock. Property grade and the ability to expand or modify the house may also be key factors. Buyers will also want to consider if a classic sandy beach is desired, as certain parts of our lake have a natural sandy shoreline, while other parts tend to have muddy clay soil.

Keep in mind that regulations may prevent buyers from performing updates at some properties, so its really important to have a real estate professional who knows those regulations and can help determine if a prospective property can meet the buyer's needs. For instance, most of our waterfront property has a 50-foot lake buffer (starting at the high water mark) that was established when the property was deeded back in the 1970s. Despite this, many houses have been built within that area because the county didn't recognize the building restrictions and gave out permits to build the houses anyway. Properties with such issues could prevent the buyer from getting title insurance, so this is critical to discover before closing. It would also be an obstacle when the buyer wants to resell in the future and might require a lengthy variance process. The 50-foot buffer requirement can also prevent expansion or the ability to add another element (such as a pool) between the house and the lake if the house is already too close. Buyers should also be aware that some subdivisions impose a larger buffer zone.

After negotiations are completed and a purchase contract is signed, buyers need to complete due diligence on the property within the specified period. We have a list of recommended vendors for the various inspections and surveys that should be completed as well as attorneys and insurance agents. Structural, mechanical and termite inspections are always recommended, regardless of the specific location and they are recommended even if the house in new. Buyers should always get a survey completed on the property to make sure the exact boundaries are known and to check that the improvements conform to setback and buffer restrictions. Buyers really need to make sure that any such issues are dealt with before the close, and a property survey can provide full information. I've seen attorneys not familiar with waterfront property that allow sales to proceed and don't realize there's going to be a buffer issue down the road, so I recommend that my buyers deal with an attorney who is familiar with the lakefront property market so that this never becomes a problem in the first place

Boating is generally an important interest for waterfront buyers; therefore, a dock will be a key consideration. There are many conditions that need to be dealt with before the purchase is closed. If there is an existing dock at the property I recommend having a local dock builder come to inspect the dock to check for any unseen issues. There are a number of restrictions relating to docks that can affect the ability to build or expand a dock and even that can restrict ability to practically use a dock. When the property is located along the main part of the lake, the dock can only extend out a certain distance. In a cove, the rules are that the dock can only span one-third of the width of the cove. A dock also can't cross the line that projects outward into the cove from another property. Sometimes, because of these restrictions, a dock is stuck in pretty shallow water, and that makes it hard to dock a boat there. Many times the restrictions will also prevent putting in a boatlift, so it can be very difficult to accommodate such a dock in those situations.

Buyers coming to this area who aren't originally from outside the city often don't know that most properties here are going to be on well and septic instead of city services. This could affect the ability to expand the property, and makes it really important that due diligence is done on the septic system. Septic systems are permitted to accommodate a certain number of bedrooms, so it's important that the residence not be expanded beyond what the septic system was designed for without also upgrading the septic. There have been some regulations in the last few years against marketing a home as containing a certain number of bedrooms if the septic can't support it, but a lot of the time the septic isn't actually approved for the number of existing bedrooms. A lot of lake properties were originally small riverfront cabins so the septic was only made for 2 or 3 bedrooms, but people tore them down and put up their 5-bedroom dream homes.

Even if the property checks out when it's being purchased, owners still have to be careful when upgrading. If the purchase is for an undeveloped lot, there are regulations about how close the septic can be to the lake and of course the design has to support the planned number of bedrooms and the type of soil on the property.

One other consideration for buyers to keep in mind is that waterfront properties do need a bit more upkeep because of the reflection off the water, which will affect the exterior siding and the time between maintenance.

With all of the considerations especially for waterfront properties, buyers should find a real estate agent who knows the area and the special considerations for waterfront property really well. Such an agent will know which parts of the lake, for instance, are shallow and which are deep, or which parts are filling in with sediment, such as the northern end and some of the coves. Some parts of the lake have that more classic sandy beach line, so if the buyer is looking for that special place for the kids and grandkids to play, that should be kept in mind. Properties right on the channel get more waves beating up the shoreline, while properties back in coves have reduced views, so it's all about what a buyer wants. A qualified real estate agent can also help with more specific considerations about a property, such as its size, its grade (flat or steep), how hard it is to get back up from the dock and so on, and their expertise will help narrow down the options. I'm always willing to work with buyers until they find that perfect home or undeveloped property they're looking for. Overall Lake Wylie is a beautiful place to buy your home.

What Buyers Are Saying:

"Honest and knowledgeable. There is not another realtor my wife or I would use ... and I have a relative in the business! Andy showed us a number of homes and always pointed out the pros and cons of each location. We never felt pressured at any time, as Andy handled all of the details of the transaction from initial showings thru the closing. We

highly recommend Andy, whether buying or selling, as he has also sold two houses for us."

-Dick B.

"Andy helped us purchase our first home. He was wonderful with the entire process from start to finish. He would answer every question we had and even gave us advice on different things to look for in the house hunt. Certain things we never would have thought about like thinking about water bills in certain areas vs. others or electric bills in homes with vaulted ceilings; he made sure we were educated about everything. Andy made the entire experience painless and enjoyable for us. He has even stayed in contact over a year later and checks in every now and again to make sure we are doing well. He remains accessible to ask questions, which is wonderful ... right down to recommendations for a plumber, etc. Andy is such an asset to the Lake Wylie community! He is a wonderful Realtor and man. I would recommend him to anyone looking to buy and/or sell."

-Lynn

Featured Lake Wylie Neighborhoods

Woodland Bay
Woodland Bay is a gated lakefront luxury community on South New Hope Road along Lake Wylie in Belmont. Woodland Bay has a natural setting and large lake channel views. The lots are large, heavily wooded and most are on the waterfront. The development has community boat slips available for owners with interior lots. Home values generally range from $500,000 to $1.7 million.

Misty Waters
Misty Waters is an upscale, gated community on Lake Wylie in Belmont. The development is located at one of the most tranquil spots on Lake Wylie and features large, wooded lots. Amenities include a community clubhouse and pool. Community boat docks are also available for homeowners not directly on the water. Interior homes range from $450,000 to $600,000 and waterfront home range over $1 million.

The Sanctuary
The Sanctuary, located on the Charlotte, North Carolina side of the lake features very large lots of 2 to 13 acres. Two hundred acres of the development are devoted to natural areas. Homeowner amenities are extensive and include a clubhouse, pool, fitness center, tennis and a boating center. There are more than 20 miles of nature trails available to residents. Home values range from $750,000 to over $2 million.

Reflection Pointe
Reflection Pointe is a large gated community along the lake in Belmont. The community offers a pool, tennis, recreation fields and walking trails. There are community boat slips available for property owners without direct access to the water. Homes off of the water start at $500,000 and lakefront homes range from $800,000 to $2 million.

Handsmill on Lake Wylie
Handsmill on Lake Wylie features abundant open space and is located on the South Carolina side of the lake. It is a large gated community with a pool, fitness center, clubhouse and playground available for residents. There are nature trails and a marina for property owners without waterfront property. Interior homes are valued from $400,000 to $500,000 and waterfront homes range from $1 million to $2 million.

The Landing
The Landing is on the South Carolina side of Lake Wylie near the middle of the main channel. The development features walking trails and a community pool. Community boat docks are available for owners without waterfront properties. Home values start around $300,000 for properties off of the water and are from $650,000 to $900,000 on the waterfront.

River Hills Plantation
River Hills Plantation is a large planned development in South Carolina near the Buster Boyd Bridge. It is a gated community with its own private security force. The centerpiece is the River Hills Country Club. Amenities include a golf course, tennis, a fitness center, walking paths, parks and a marina club. River Hills has a diverse range of properties from condos starting at $180,000 to waterfront estates valued at $1.6 million.

Tega Cay
Tega Cay is a planned lakefront city with a South Seas theme situated on a peninsula at the south end of Lake Wylie. Tega Cay has 13 miles of shoreline and is generally heavily wooded and with rolling hills. There is a 27-hole public golf course and a marina is available for homeowners without waterfront property. The city offers numerous natural walking trails and lakefront parks. Interior home are available in Tega Cay

starting at $200,000 and lakefront home range up to $2 million.

Riverpointe
Riverpointe is a large, heavily wooded community on the North Carolina side of the lake just north of the Buster Boyd Bridge. The development offers a pool, tennis, a playground and walking trails. There is also a marina for residents living off of the water. Interior homes start at $300,000 and waterfront homes range up to $1.5 million.

Joslin Pointe
Joslin Point is a small and exclusive gated development at the south end of Lake Wylie in Rock Hill. The community of European styled homes offers mostly waterfront properties with expansive lake views. There is a private beach as well as a pool and clubhouse for use by residents. Home values range from $780,000 to $2 million.

About Andy Reynolds

Andy Reynolds is the top ranked Keller Williams agent in the greater Lake Wylie area and is ranked in the top one percent of all Keller Williams agents in the Carolinas Region. He has been representing buyers and sellers in real estate transactions since 2006 and is licensed in both North Carolina and South Carolina.

Andy's expertise derives from many sources, including a lifetime spent on Lake Wylie and a background in boat sales at the lake. He has helped numerous buyers and sellers realize their real estate goals, and as a Certified Negotiation Expert is able to expertly negotiate on his clients' behalf at the closing table and in all types of real estate transaction. He especially enjoys helping families to find their dream homes along the Lake Wylie waterfront.

A member of the Piedmont Realtors Association and the Charlotte Realtors Association, Andy is also an elected and serving member of the local Keller Williams office's Associates Leadership Council. His motto is, "From sign up to sign down, I work for you."

For more information about Andy Reynolds and how to work with him, visit his website at http://www.andyonlakewylie.com.

Chapter 3

Sam Grogan

Luxury Properties

I have been helping buyers and sellers with property sales and purchases in the Charlotte area since 2001. I knew I was going to love this profession when I was helping my first clients in 2001, a family that needed to relocate due to having a difficult time with a family member's health issues. They happily make one of the most important decisions, buying a home in the area, and their outlook had completely been transformed away from the stresses they were experiencing.

Although I work with buyers and sellers in the full range of property values in the greater Charlotte area, I am a Previews® Certified agent with Coldwell Banker. This is a designation for agents certified to represent buyers and sellers in the top ten percent of home values, essentially luxury properties. I take a lot of pride in being trained and equipped to provide exceptional service to high net worth buyers and sellers.

Charlotte has been a real hot spot for companies relocating to the area due to the attractive business environment, the relatively low cost of commercial real estate, the availability of a great employee talent and the moderate climate. My team works with a large number of relocation buyers ranging from mid-level management all the way up to company owners and CEO's. In addition to the relocation clientele, we also represent many local move-up buyers, looking to upgrade from their existing homes. Charlotte's beautiful lake communities also attract a lot of vacation homebuyers and even local weekend homebuyers looking for the perfect weekend retreat.

Selling Your Charlotte Area Luxury Home

When first meeting with a luxury homeowner, the initial point raised is almost always the expected pricing. With luxury homes, generally above one million dollars in the greater Charlotte area, the properties are all unique, so research is required to establish a proper value. We use a two–step approach when working with high value properties. During the first meeting, I will familiarize myself with the property, look at all of the features, take measurements and review all of the upgrades and the designer touches. We will also want to understand the owner's timing considerations. This is the starting point for the pricing analysis and later when I return for the next meeting I will provide the pricing analysis as well as the custom marketing plan for the property.

More research is required to properly define the value of a custom luxury home compared with valuation in a production-built community, where there may be eight or ten floor plans and some variations on features, but the values are all similar within the community. When analyzing luxury properties we will look at comparable sales with similar square footage, similar features, similar property acreage, number of bedrooms and bathrooms and we typically have to go a bit farther away to find enough comparable property sales.

Inventory and absorption rate are import to understand in pricing a luxury property. Absorption is the number of similar homes selling within a month, but is computed by looking at sales over the past year and dividing by twelve. Let's say the inventory of similar homes on the market is fifty and the absorption rate is ten homes per month, the average time on market would be five months. Depending on the needs of the owners, pricing can generally be more aggressive, with a higher price, if the months of inventory are lower, such a two months compared with a higher inventory of say eight months.

After completing the research we will meet with the owners a second time to review our pricing analysis as well as to present the custom marketing program that we suggest for the property. During the review, we discuss the designer and other unique features of the property and comparable properties and the price per square foot for other similar homes that have sold in the same area or similar areas. We discuss these all in terms of value and then we discuss the absorption rate, the number of showings that are going on in the specific price range of the property and we summarize our pricing research and conclusions, leading to a recommended price for the property.

We continue the meeting with a description of our marketing program to expose the property to the highest number of buyers. Exposure is really the key to a successful sale, particularly for higher priced properties. Each luxury property is unique and has its own personality and aura. In marketing the home, it is important to showcase the unique qualities, unique features and personal story of the home. If done properly, there is a dramatic increase in the ability to attract multiple prospective buyers.

Our marketing presentation spells out our marketing strategy and everything we will be doing from start to finish. For luxury homes this will include custom photography, a virtual tour, exposure on multiple real estate websites and YouTube. High value homes need quality professional photography to properly demonstrate the style, features and amenities. We will bring in a professional photographer, even if it takes a few more days, to properly showcase the home. Technology has advanced to the point where we can incorporate aerial drone footage in the videos. We will also elaborate all of the designer and name brand features and upgrades, including appliances and built-in electronics. A three-tiered media approach is used to present the property to prospective buyers. They see the video, there is a text description and the video has a voice-over describing the property to them. There are dual benefits with this as it engages the consumers that see something they like and it disengages viewers that see something that's maybe not ideal for their specific needs. The idea behind this is not only to have a quantity with respect to showings, but we also want to have quality showings to interested potential buyers. In essence the buyers that do come through the door have seen something they like and want to investigate further.

Prospective sellers should start talking with an agent as soon as they begin to consider selling their house. We can provide recommendations that may actually save money, time and effort. Some owners think the home has to be completely de-personalized before starting the process and they go too far. We really want the property to feel like a home so when a prospective buyer walks in the door, it looks like a loved, cared for and happy place. The home should be neat and clean and staged properly so it's not overbearing. First impressions are absolutely critical, as people tend, to within the first five to ten steps into a property, know if it's not going to fit what they are looking for. Make sure that the entry way or foyer is neat and clean and smells fresh and for a single-family home that the landscaping is all in order.

Some luxury home sellers have the misconception that all real estate agents are the same. This couldn't be further from the truth and I would recommend sellers to verify the agent's qualifications to properly market a luxury property. They should inquire as to the prospective agent's experience and quantity of successfully closed high value property sales. Past client testimonials are also a good indicator and should be reviewed. Sellers should expect that an agent can logically rationalize the pricing proposal as well as describe the specific marketing program the agent will use to expose the property to the most potential buyers. Also the agent should be able to provide examples of successes with the marketing plan being described.

Everyone knows a real estate agent or knows someone that does. That doesn't mean the agent is the best advisor to a luxury client. One indicator of capability is if the agent has a certification from the realty company that indicates a level of training and experience with serving luxury property clients. As a seller, you want to choose an agent that will provide you with a plenty of confidence that the agent will have the ability to handle representation on a high value property.

A consideration that often arises with our listings is when a buyer sees our advertising and contacts us directly to inquire about a property we have listed. Although Dual Agency, where the same agent represents both a buyer and a seller in a transaction, is legal, I will only represent one side of the transaction. I firmly believe that an agent can only properly represent the seller or the buyer in a transaction, not both. When a seller lists with me, my commitment to the seller is to try to get the highest price for the home. Likewise when a buyer works with me to purchase a home, my promise is to negotiate the best possible price and terms for the buyer. By definition, it is impossible to do both. My policy is to only represent one party to a transaction. If the situation arises where a buyer contacts me to show them one of my listings, I refer the buyer to a different member of our team, so each of us can properly represent the buyer and the seller. This leads to a question sellers should be asking up front when they are considering listing with an agent – whether the agent will be bringing buyers to make an offer. I recommend that sellers make sure they understand before listing who will be representing them if the agent also brings a buyer and I suggest that sellers only work with an agent that will not represent both at the same time.

What Sellers Are Saying:

"We were introduced to Sam as he represented our next door neighbors in the sale of their property. The sale of their

property was exceedingly successful. We felt strongly that he was capable of representing us well in the sale of our property from his very professional and assertive approach with our neighbors.

Sam was proactive, responsive and engaged throughout the process. His recommendations on pricing were compelling and supportable and the marketing strategy was comprehensive and aggressive. We ultimately sold for a price that was very satisfying, but most importantly he helped our family manage the situation in the midst of a challenging travel schedule, an infant and a pregnancy. We have and will continue to refer him to others."

- Jason and Carol B.

"My wife and I were faced with a variety of challenges as we prepared to list our condo in Uptown Charlotte. I had taken a new job in Atlanta, which required we relocate in a very tight timeframe of about a month. In addition, the real estate market for luxury condos in Charlotte was not robust at the time, with many units remaining on the market for well over 6 months, or were sold for steep discounts from asking. To top it off, there were three other identical units for sale on our floor. Needless to say, finding the right real estate partner was our top priority. We interviewed three agents for our listing and, while each presented a compelling case, Sam Grogan stood out. Sam made us feel comfortable and confident not only because of his experience, expertise and creativity, but most importantly because of his practical, down to earth and genuine approach and style.

The best part for us was that Sam delivered on what he pitched. Sam was hands on and proactive from day one. He personally managed all aspects of marketing from photography to immediate advertisements in the top Charlotte magazines. He also had very specific buyers lined up in advance and wasted no time securing showings.

Sam's efforts paid off, as we were able to sell our home in 3 days for above asking price. Sam is a pleasure to work with, a true professional. We can't imagine a better partner and advisor."

- Emory and Theresa T.

Buying Your Charlotte Area Luxury Property

The Charlotte area has a wide variety of attractive luxury neighborhoods. We have several high-rise condominium buildings in the Uptown or Center City area with spacious units and beautiful city views. There are some near-to Uptown neighborhoods with tree-lined streets and historic estate homes. The popular south Charlotte area has many luxury neighborhoods, several adjoining some of the region's top golf and country clubs. One example, Quail Hollow Club, has one of the top golf courses in the country and is home to one of the top annual PGA Tour events and is also the site of the 2017 PGA Championship and the 2021 Presidents Cup, two of the most prestigious events in professional golf. Charlotte also has three large lakes with a combined 900 miles of shoreline and many dozens of luxury neighborhoods. Waterfront resort living at one of the lakes is possible with an easy commute into the city.

Most local move-up clients generally are quite familiar with the region and know the general area where they want to look for a house. Many luxury buyers from outside the Charlotte area are moving with large corporate relocations into the area. My first step in working with relocation clients is to get an understanding of some key requirements, such as price range, lifestyle preferences and the maximum time or distance range to the workplace or airport. Lifestyle considerations would include such interests as boating, golf and proximity to cultural events, shopping and restaurants. We also want to know the basic requirements such as minimum square footage, number of bedrooms and type of

43

community, such as a single-family home, a condominium or in a planned development. By knowing the lifestyle preferences, the work location and their preference for maximum commute time we can identify a range of appropriate neighborhoods to visit to get a better view of client preferences. Once a range of neighborhoods is identified, we can develop a list of available properties to view. By interviewing the client and getting an upfront understanding of their requirements, we can save a lot of the buyer's time and focus on neighborhoods and properties that will meet their needs.

Relocation buyers seeking a luxury residence will want to make sure they select an agent who has experience in the entire Charlotte area. Otherwise, appropriate neighborhoods and properties might be totally overlooked and the client will not be well represented. As with the luxury home seller, it is recommended to work with an agent that is qualified to negotiate for the high value properties. Experience can be determined by certifications, such as certification to represent luxury property buyers and sellers, by the amount of closed transactions of high values properties on both the buying and selling side and by reviewing past client testimonials. Experience and certifications for working with relocation clients are other important considerations. It is important that in addition to the skill level of the agent, the buyer is working with someone they feel they can trust and is confident that the agent has the buyer's best interest at heart. It is very important to have a good rapport with the agent. We are probably among the least pushy of real estate agents and our interest is to truly develop long-term relationships with our clients.

Before making an offer on a property, the buyer will want to determine if there are any restrictions on use of the property through Home Owner's Association (HOA) regulations or CC&Rs (Covenants, Conditions & Restrictions) on the development or on the specific property. Many times these types of restrictions can limit what can be done with the property and may possibly prohibit certain expansions or modifications, development of additional buildings, such as a second living residence on the property, fencing, landscaping design and other possible limitations. Clearly if the restrictions would inhibit a buyer's future intended use, the property would not be suitable.

Once a property is selected, an offer is submitted and negotiated, and an agreement is made with a seller, it is time for the buyer to complete final due diligence on the property. Generally the same recommendations apply regardless of the property value. We have recommended resources that are qualified to undertake legal work, inspections, surveys and other tests. Our recommended inspectors perform a full range of structural and mechanical system inspections as well as termite inspections, which are important in this area. Although radon is not a common problem, we recommend a radon test, especially with houses that have imported granite or other stone and homes with basements. We always recommend a survey to verify the exact property boundaries and to determine if there are any hidden pitfalls such as recorded stump holes. Especially for larger properties, buyers will want to see if there are any encroachments on the property or any easements that might be present. Buyers certainly want to know how much of what they are viewing will be their property. Some luxury properties, especially around the lakes and in unincorporated areas, have a well and septic tank instead of city services. In this case we will also recommend that the buyer get a septic inspection and a well water quality test. Back in the 1990's and 2000's there was a lot of synthetic stucco used, particularly on expensive houses in the area. There were issues with some synthetic stucco installations, so that would be another recommended inspection point if the property has synthetic stucco facing.

Title insurance will be required if there will be a loan on the property and we would recommend title insurance even for a property purchased for cash. The closing attorney will perform the title search and sign off on good title. One potential difference with an all cash purchase is that an appraisal is not required; in fact it may not be of particular use. Luxury properties are rather unique and the negotiation sets the price and it is unlikely the seller will negotiate if the appraisal comes in lower than the agreed price.

What Buyers Are Saying:

"We first met Sam through a real estate agent we had used to sell our house in Dallas, Texas. He came highly recommended and for good reason. Normally, we like to interview numerous real estate agents but it was clear early on that Sam would be our only choice to buy in the Charlotte area. He was extremely knowledgeable and involved throughout the buying process. He would point out both strengths and weaknesses in properties we visited and provided essential inputs in our decision making process. In fact, with Sam's knowledge we were able to avoid purchasing at least two properties we were initially very interested in and which, in hindsight, we are now extremely thankful to have avoided. We have and will continue to refer him to anyone looking to purchase in the luxury housing market in Charlotte. We certainly cannot imagine making such an important investment decision without Sam in our corner."

- Glyn and Christi W.

"My wife and I worked with Sam Grogan at Coldwell Banker on a relocation from Sarasota, Florida to the greater Charlotte area. We absolutely loved working with Sam. He guided us through the process of locating the best area in Charlotte that met our specific needs. We never felt pressured to 'settle' for a place we didn't love. Sam took us all over the metro Charlotte Region and really gave us a good idea and feel for the area. This helped us find the right location for our family. Sam made the experience, which is inherently stressful, actually a lot of fun. Sam was always

super quick to respond, really on top of everything, and went way above and beyond for us. He's totally professional. On top of that, he's just a really great guy, funny, and we genuinely enjoyed working with him, and getting to know him. We ended up buying a house in a beautiful country club in South Charlotte. I would highly recommend Sam and can honestly say that after 6 home purchases Sam is one of the best realtors we have ever dealt with!"

- *Dean and Candy R.*

Featured Luxury Neighborhoods and Areas

Ballantyne Country Club
Ballantyne Country Club is just off of I-485 in South Charlotte near Hwy 521 and is part of the master-planned Ballantyne development. Walkers, runners and bikers abound on the lush landscaped streets and wide sidewalks. The residential areas are built around and near the Rees Jones designed championship golf course and its luxurious clubhouse, swim club and tennis courts. Many restaurants and shopping centers are close by within Ballantyne. Home prices range from the mid $500,000s to over $2 million.

Myers Park
Myers Park is an historic luxury subdivision started in the early 1900's, just south of Uptown Charlotte. It has Old South charm with New South amenities, close to the Center City and minutes from SouthPark and other shopping centers. Mature oak tree lined streets and majestic main street residences give way to quiet side streets and lovely bungalows. Myers Park Country Club's golf course is an original Donald Ross layout that has been recently renovated. Home prices in the area range from the mid $200,000s to over $3 million.

Quail Hollow Club Area
There are a number of residential developments adjacent to and near the Quail Hollow Club, which is in South Charlotte, not far from SouthPark and numerous business parks. There is something for everyone in the area from split-level homes built in the 1960's to large estates within gated communities. Shopping and restaurants are nearby. The Quail Hollow Club's golf course is one of the highest rated in the country and is well known as the host of the annual PGA tour event and it will be the home of the 2017 PGA Championship as well as the 2021 Presidents Cup. Homes in the area range from the high $200,000s to over $3 million.

Eastover

Eastover is an historic neighborhood started in the 1920's of almost exclusively single-family homes adjacent to Myers Park and just to the Southeast of Uptown Charlotte. The neighborhood has some of Charlotte's most stately homes along mature tree-lined and winding streets. Restaurants and shopping are on the edge of the neighborhood and SouthPark and several other shopping centers are nearby. Home prices range from the $300,000s to over $4 million.

Uptown Condominiums

Center City, or Uptown Charlotte, has several condominium buildings and most of them have penthouse luxury units. Uptown is home to over 100,000 jobs and the condo complexes are all within walking distance to the office buildings and the many amenities such as top-rated restaurants, sports and music venues, nightclubs and museums. Shopping within the Uptown area is somewhat limited, but there are several neighborhood centers nearby and SouthPark is only about 10 to 15 minutes away. Uptown condo pricing starts around $200,000 and penthouse units range up to over $2 million.

Carmel Country Club Area

There are several residential neighborhoods along and around Carmel Country Club, just off of Carmel Road in South Charlotte. These neighborhoods are just minutes from SouthPark and all of the shopping and restaurants as well as many business parks. Carmel County Club has two 18-hole golf courses, swimming and tennis. The South Course was recently redeveloped by Rees Jones. There are a variety of older and new neighborhoods in the Carmel Club area with prices ranging from the $200,000s to over $2 million.

The Club at Longview

The Club at Longview is an exclusive gated community south of I-485, just into Union County to the South of Charlotte. Shopping and restaurants are nearby at Blakney and Ballantyne, just minutes away. Longview is an easy commute to many business parks and Uptown Charlotte. The community has a 24-hour staffed gatehouse and is surrounding a Jack Nicklaus Signature championship golf course. Home prices range from the $700,000s to several million dollars.

Piper Glen

Piper Glen is a golf course community in South Charlotte just North of I-485 along Rea Road. There is an abundance of shopping and restaurants in the immediate vicinity and it is also just minutes from SouthPark, Ballantyne and several business parks. Residential developments surround the TPC Piper Glen golf course designed by Arnold Palmer. The club also offers a pool and tennis. The neighborhood is heavily wooded and offers walking trails. Home prices start in the upper $300,000s to over $2 million.

Morrocroft Estates

Morrocroft Estates is a luxury gated community in the SouthPark area. Shopping, restaurants and everything that SouthPark has to offer are nearby, even within walking distance. It's just a short drive to Uptown Charlotte and to many business parks. With most homes on an acre or more, the neighborhood offers privacy, right in the heart of a busy area. Gatehouses are staffed with security 24 hours per day. Prices in Morrocroft start in the $900,000s and some properties are valued over $5 million.

Lake Wylie Waterfront

With 325 miles of shoreline, Lake Wylie is along the border of North and South Carolina just to the Southwest of Charlotte. Living at the lake is like being at a vacation resort, yet it is an easy commute into Charlotte and many other business centers. There are many residential developments along the lake and shopping and restaurants are generally only minutes away. Although some residential developments along the lake have properties off the water starting from the $200,000s, waterfront homes generally start in the $700,000s and range up to over $2 million.

About Sam Grogan

Sam Grogan is a full time Real Estate Broker associated with Coldwell Banker United, Realtors in Charlotte, NC. He is licensed in both North Carolina and South Carolina and is a Previews® Certified agent with Coldwell Banker. Sam began his career in real estate in 2001 and has become one of the top performing real estate professionals in the Charlotte region. He is the founder of the Best in The Carolinas team, which has closed over 600 successful real estate transactions. The team is in the top 7% of all Coldwell Banker affiliated teams in the United States and achieved the designation of an International President's Circle Team for Coldwell Banker in 2014.

Sam and his team work with buyers and sellers in all price ranges in the greater Charlotte area. Being a Certified Previews agent, he has been trained to represent buyers and sellers in luxury property transactions, the top ten percent of home values in the market. He is also a certified e-PRO agent, keeping up to date with all of the latest technology trends in the real estate market.

For more information about Sam Grogan and the Best In The Carolinas team, visit http://BestInTheCarolinas.com. They are also on Facebook at https://www.Facebook.com/BestInTheCarolinas.

Chapter 4

Amber Garchar

Lake Norman Area Real Estate

With a background in marketing, interior design, landscaping and home staging, I started helping buyers and sellers with their real estate transactions in 2007. I really enjoy helping others and my background in these related fields gave me some well-rounded experience that benefits my clients, whether they are interested in selling their property or they are looking for a home in the area. Lake Norman Realty is the company I choose to align myself with because it is one of Lake Norman's premier, family owned, local agencies. The company and its associates manage to maintain a true family atmosphere with a global reach through affiliations with Who's Who in Luxury Real Estate and Leading Real Estate Companies of the World.

My family moved to the area in 2001 and lived in Huntersville, in popular Birkdale Village, before finding our dream home on the shores of Lake Norman. We really enjoy the lakeside living and all of the amenities that the entire area has to offer. Knowing the area and amenities extremely well is something that helps me to benefit both buyers and sellers. We have something for everyone and although I had the good fortune to be the listing agent for one of the most expensive and unique homes ever built in the Lake Norman area (Chateau Lyon), I enjoy meeting and assisting both buyers and sellers in the full range of property values around the lake. We work with clients in all of the Lake Norman communities including Cornelius, Davidson, Huntersville, Mooresville, Sherrills Ford, Terrell, Troutman, Statesville and Denver. We have waterfront condos starting at around $150,000 and lakefront homes valued into the multi-millions. The Charlotte region's growth has been spurred by many corporate relocations. Relocation buyers have a wide range of needs and very specific lifestyle criteria. My own experience moving here and getting to know the area is key when assisting individuals and their families on such and important move.

Selling Your Lake Norman Property

Most often potential sellers don't contact an agent until they are ready to list their house for sale. They may have planned to sell for some time and they may have made improvements or repairs they believed would help their house sell. Too many times we see potential sellers spend more than necessary or make some changes that I would not recommend. Another common mistake is to go overboard in removing clutter to the extent that the home loses any personality. My suggestion would be that anyone planning to sell within a few months to start talking with an agent as soon as possible. An experienced agent will provide upfront advice and help the seller minimize the amount of work necessary early in the process.

Proper timing to introduce a property to the market is important and depends on inventory levels and the general market situation. Though spring is traditionally the prime time of the year to list one's home, the Southeast, in particular, is not seasonally limited. Charlotte is one of the fastest growing metro areas in the United States and the growth is partly driven by the favorable business environment for corporate relocations. In recent years we are experiencing relocations year-round, not just during summer. The lake areas around Charlotte also attract those looking for a great place to retire or buy a vacation home, so not all buyers' schedules are focused around the school schedules. Throughout 2014 and into 2015 homes have been in higher demand due to relatively low inventory levels. These situations will change from year-to-year, so potential sellers should choose an experienced Realtor that really knows the market and how to advise on timing for the marketplace.

When working with homeowners interested in selling their properties, pricing is typically their main concern. Prospective sellers should expect that their Realtor will provide statistics to back up the pricing analysis and have the ability to demonstrate sound reasoning for the conclusions on proposed pricing. Location is a key parameter when determining value and pricing. Comparable sales statistics should be, whenever possible, narrowed down to the neighborhood level, not just the community level or even just the Lake Norman area level. Sellers in the Lake Norman area should strive to work with an agent that has a number of years of experience working with both buyers and sellers and is focused on the Lake Norman area.

Psychology and advice from years ago can negatively affect properly pricing a property in today's market. Let's say that a property is valued right around $500,000. Many sellers will suggest that the property be priced at $499,000 instead of $500,000, believing pricing just under $500,000 sounds better. What really happens is that many potential buyers of houses around $500,000 or more will not likely see the listing. Today most buyers do a lot of research online and the online real estate sites have ranges that the buyer must select to view properties. One common range break point is $500,000, so the sites may have a range of from $300,000 to $500,000 and from $500,000 to $750,000. If the price is set at $499,000, buyers looking for a house between $500,00 and $750,000 will not see the listing. An experienced agent will advise the seller on the proper pricing to get exposure to a wider group of potential buyers.

One thing commonly done for buyers, but which I also do for sellers, is to set up an online community market watch for activity on properties in their community and especially in their neighborhood. They will be alerted for any new activity on houses listed for sale along with pricing, photos and how many days on the market. In this way, sellers can stay aware of the real time market activity in their neighborhood.

First impressions mean a lot in attracting the largest amount of potential buyers, so sellers want to make sure that their property shows well. Usually most people need some help in identifying repairs and cosmetic changes that should be made and in de-cluttering. As an Accredited Staging Professional (ASP), I go through a house from outside to inside and room-by-room and make a list of everything that needs to be done to get the house in the best condition to expect the highest sale price. Sometimes there are repairs needed and frequently small, inexpensive cosmetic changes can be made that can put the property into a better position to compete with others. Sometimes it is not just about competing; it may help to get a higher price. Staging is really more about editing the furnishings and decorations within the house. I do not advise to completely de-personalize the house as buyers still want to get a sense of what it will be like to live in it when it becomes their home. My professional staging advice is included for my selling clients at no additional fee.

As a seller, you don't want to have surprises before the closing from unseen repairs that may be needed. All buyers are going to be having an inspection completed prior to closing. My view is that it is better to have through knowledge of the property condition and confidence in the structure and its mechanical systems prior to the buyer conducting their inspection. My recommendation is that sellers have their own inspection performed prior to listing and marketing their home. When you have lived in a house for many years, there are sometimes things owners don't notice because of familiarity. It is better to know in advance than to find out there is an issue after you are under contract and potentially lose a buyer.

In summary, make sure your agent has several successful years of experience with Lake Norman area properties and can demonstrate a history of successful completed transactions. Look for testimonials from past clients and make sure the agent provides good logic and reasoning for the proposed pricing. Your agent should provide a marketing plan for exposing the property to the largest amount of potential buyers. Using the advice of an accredited home stager will give some comfort that your furnishings and decorations will present a great first impression to prospective buyers.

What Sellers Are Saying:

"I recently worked with Amber to sell my house on Lake Norman. Amber was able to give me an accurate market value and moved the home within six weeks at close to the asking price. The home sold at one of the highest sales values for the neighborhood. She went out of her way to ensure the house was staged properly and in show condition while I was out of state. As part of the sale, she worked with the buyers to value the furniture and include it in the sale, as I did not want to move it.

Amber's responsiveness to phone calls and emails and knowledge of the intricacies of my particular situation made the process smooth and timely. She continued to assist me post-sale with the transition to the new owners. I would highly recommend Amber as a real estate agent for anyone looking to get the most for their home."

- Robert I.

"Amber Garchar went above and beyond the call of duty to help get our townhome sold. She stuck with us every step of the way. She was meticulous and patient in answering all of our questions and concerns. I loved how persistent she was in getting feedback from the clients that visited our home. When searching for a home to purchase, she truly listened to our needs and helped us find the perfect home for our family. Amber was also able to recommend contractors for

projects when we purchased our new home as well. She has kept in touch with us after the sale to check in, which I believe says a lot about the kind of person she is. I highly recommend calling Amber if you're looking for someone to help guide you through the process, address your concerns, and help you seal the deal in a very competitive market! She is a true professional in every sense of the word, and puts her clients' interests above her own."

- Jason & Jemma C.

Buying Your Lake Norman Property

The first piece of advise I have for buyers would be to speak with several lenders (mortgage companies), explore which rates, programs and service levels they prefer and select one they feel comfortable and confident working with. Their lender should ensure the buyer knows the amount of loan that the buyer will qualify for. Buyers make a much better impression to sellers when they are pre-qualified and this can make a buyer's offer more appealing than a non pre-qualified buyer's offer. I have several experienced and trusted mortgage professionals that I can refer to buyers if they need assistance with financing. At Lake Norman Realty we actually have an in-house lender, on-site at our Cornelius branch, to assist with a one-stop home buying experience.

Lake Norman is a large lake with 520 miles of shoreline and many communities in the area to consider. A buyer interested in the Lake Norman area should definitely work with an experienced Realtor that specializes in the lake area. Once a buyer has a good understanding of the price range of properties they will be considering, I then like to spend some time with them discussing other considerations, such as home size, wants/needs, distance to schools, work, medical services, shopping and restaurants. Other important things I like to consider are buyers' hobbies such as golf, tennis and water activities, as I want to ensure their new home will provide access to these.

Waterfront properties present many different considerations for a buyer and an experienced lake area Realtor will be able to help the buyer understand the differences and trade offs. There are restrictions at the lake to keep all permanent structures at least fifty feet from the waterline and some communities have even greater restrictions. If a buyer plans to construct a swimming pool or wants to expand the house, it is advisable to check first to see if there is room beyond the setback requirements for such structures. Many properties at the lake have a septic system so it is also recommended to understand when purchasing, the location of the septic system to make sure it will not interfere with any planned construction of a pool or other residence expansion.

Many of our buyers are especially interested in boating, so it is important to be able to assist them with docking/storage options. We really need to understand current and future buyer preferences as they relate to boating. Sailing, for example, is a popular activity at the lake and so buyers interested in having a sailboat docked on their property need to consider their boat. Some coves may be too shallow; in addition, there are some bridges that a sailboat may not fit under and could restrict access to the main channel of the lake. If a buyer is interested in having a dock on their waterfront property and one is not already in place, it will be necessary to check regulations to ensure one can be permitted. The water level fluctuates at different times of the year so some properties may not be suitable to dock a boat when the levels recede. Also, boat wakes and waves can cause wear and tear if your property is on the much-traveled main channel of the lake so a boatlift may need to be a consideration.

After the buyer works with the agent to make an offer and the purchase is negotiated, it is time to conduct inspections and other due diligence. Regardless of the location, buyers will want to have structural and mechanical system inspections conducted by an experienced inspector. Termite inspections are also necessary in this area. A survey of the property is also recommended to confirm conformance to all of the setback restrictions. If there is an existing dock, the dock should be inspected and a check should also be made to ensure that the dock was properly permitted when it was constructed, as it is not uncommon to find issues. If there is no existing dock and the buyer is interested in constructing a dock, make sure to check if a dock is feasible and can be permitted, if not already checked.

As previously mentioned, many of our lake area properties have a septic system, so I recommend that the septic system be inspected. Many properties also have a well for water supply, and if that is the case with the property being purchased, a well water test would also be recommended. If there is a septic system, make sure the location of the tank and field is known, as there cannot be any future construction over these areas.

Relocation buyers will want to consider if the agent will be willing and available to coordinate inspections and other critical due diligence functions while the buyers are out of town. That is something that I happily do for buyers, but not all agents may be accommodating is this area.

What Buyers Are Saying:

"It is with pleasure and gratitude that we share comments on our experience with Amber Garchar while representing us for the search and purchase of our home.

Amber is extremely professional, reliable, patient and exceptionally honest. Her ability to understand our needs made the whole experience a pleasurable one. In our personal opinion, a real estate agent like Amber is a rare find.

The experience at each phase of the search, and subsequent purchase, was superior. Her innovative efforts in developing prospective neighborhood targets, her useful insights on renovations/decorating, her effective route mapping and proactive facilitation during the negotiations were exceptional. All of these tasks, whether business-related or interpersonal, were accomplished with a noticeable degree of competence, humility, integrity and grace.

Amber went above and beyond to make sure that we found the right home for our family and we highly recommend her for all of your residential real estate needs."

Don & Amanda K.

"It is my personal honor to sing the praises of Amber Garchar, a competent professional and instant friend. She emailed listings daily to my son living in New York and moving to the Lake Norman area due to a job transfer. He was in North Carolina for three days and she found him the perfect home. I followed two months later and in a single day she found us exactly the ranch home we were looking for in the exact area and with the three-car garage that was a priority for us. She was thorough, polite, professional and personable. She went way beyond what was required, handling the closing so we did not have to be there and even arranging for floors and carpeting to be installed before our arrival. I look forward to inviting Amber over to our home as she was definitely the first friend we made here in North Carolina."

- Vita G.

Featured Lake Norman Neighborhoods and Areas

The Peninsula
The Peninsula is a large planned development spanning 11 miles of Lake Norman shoreline off of Jetton Road in Cornelius, just north of Charlotte. The development is near I-77 Exit 28 which is surrounded with shopping and restaurants and is near the 105 acre Jetton Park. The Peninsula is one of the more exclusive developments on Lake Norman, with lakefront resort-style living. The development includes a Rees Jones designed golf course overlooking the lake, a 35,000 Sq. ft. clubhouse, a yacht club, pool, pro shop, tennis and fitness center. Home prices range from the $400,000s to the multi-millions.

The Point
The Point spans 18 miles of Lake Norman's shoreline and is located near I-77 Exits 31 through 36, about 30 minutes from Uptown Charlotte. A wide variety of shopping and restaurants are located near the interstate exits. Life at The Point revolves around the water and living in the community feels like a permanent vacation. The Point is the home of Trump National Golf Club, which features a Greg Norman designed golf course with incredible views of the lake. There are three swimming pools, a fitness center, pro shop, day spa, tennis courts, a tavern, a bakery and Village green with soccer fields and a meeting house. Home prices range from the $600,000s to the multi-millions.

The Farms
The Farms community is close to the crossroads of I-77 and I-40 in Iredell County, 25 minutes north of Charlotte. Shopping and restaurants are just minutes away at Exit 36 on I-77. The community features large lots and living there feels like being in the countryside, with an abundance of space and mature wooded areas. The community features the Homestead Amenities Center, a swimming pool, tennis courts, activity fields, play ground, picnic areas and a full-

time activities director. Home prices range from the $500,000s to the high $800,000s.

Sailview
Sailview is on Lake Norman's Westside, just 30 minutes from Uptown Charlotte in Denver. Shopping and restaurants are 10 minutes away along the Hwy 73 corridor. Sailview is perfect for those with an active lifestyle. There is a Swim and Tennis Club overlooking Lake Norman, an eight-acre park with a playground and exercise station, walking paths and community boat slips. Home prices range from the $350,000s to up to the $2 millions.

Governor's Island
Governor's Island is also on Lake Norman's Westside, 30 minutes from Uptown Charlotte in Denver. The community is a private, gated island with bridge access to a narrow peninsula of palatial estates. Shopping and restaurants are 10 minutes away along the Hwy 73 corridor. The Governor's Island development has some of the best views on the lake. Home prices are $1 million plus.

Town of Cornelius
Cornelius is centered near Exit 28 of I-77. The west side of Cornelius is on the Lake Norman shoreline. There are a variety of stores and restaurants, 10 public parks, a championship golf course (at the Peninsula), bass fishing tournaments and public access to the lake. Popular Cornelius communities include Robbins Park (mid $400,000s to mid $700,000s), Antiquity (high $100,000s to mid $500,000s), Caldwell Station (mid $100,000s to high $200,000s), Blue Stone Harbor (mid $200,000s to $500,000s), Patrick's Purchase (high $600,000s to $2 Million).

Town of Davidson
Davidson is just north of Cornelius and extends from the shoreline of Lake Norman to the southeast. Interstate access is from Exit 30 of I-77. Davidson has a quaint downtown area with pedestrian-friendly streets, a farmer's market,

Mom and Pop shops, Davidson College, Lake Davidson Nature Preserve, a variety of restaurants, lakeside dining and Davidson Green. Popular communities include River Run (from the mid $300,000s to the millions), The Woodlands (the low $400,000s to the low $800,000s), Summer's Walk (the low $100,000s to the high $300,000s), Anniston (the $400,000s to the high $800,000s) and Bailey Springs (the mid $200,000s to the high $400,000s).

Town of Huntersville
Huntersville is on the southeast edge of Lake Norman centered around Exits 23 and 25 of I-77. Huntersville has a small town feel, yet is close to the city. The town has undergone one of the most impressive transformations in the state, evolving from a sleepy farming area into a job center boasting 40,000 people. Huntersville is in the midst of it all - modern shopping centers and a wide variety of restaurants. The town also has top-notch medical facilities and access to Lake Norman, Latta Plantation and Discovery Place Kids. Popular communities include Birkdale Village ($200,000s to high $300,000s), Birkdale (mid $200,000s to high $500,000s), Vermillion (high $100,000s to high $400,000s), Northstone ($200,000s to low $500,000s) and Monteith Park (mid $100,000s to high $300,000s).

Town of Mooresville
Mooresville is on the northeast edge of Lake Norman with access from Exits 31 through 36 of I-77. Mooresville combines the appeal of a small town life with easy access to cultural and sporting events in Charlotte and Winston-Salem. The town has a historic downtown district, many shopping centers, lakeside dining, restaurants, lake access points, recreation centers and parks. Mooresville is the home base for many NASCAR teams and hosts the annual Race City Festival. Popular communities include Alexander Island ($800,000s to the multi-millions), Harbour at the Pointe ($300,000s to $2 million), Shavenders Bluff ($300,000s to $600,000s), Sisters Cove ($800,000s to $1.3 million), Pinnacle Shores (high $200,000s to $1.8 million).

North Lake Area Communities of Troutman, Sherrills Ford and Statesville

Troutman, Sherrills Ford and Statesville are at the north end of Lake Norman and are experiencing continuing growth. They are in close proximity to Mooresville, which has a large variety of shopping and restaurants. The north lake communities are relaxed and laid back and are great for nature lovers and active outdoor lifestyles. Lake Norman State Park is a popular destination along the north shore of the lake. Popular communities include Northview Harbour in Sherrills Ford (mid $300,000s to multi-millions), Wildlife Bay in Troutman (mid $200,000s to mid $800,000s), Harbor Watch in Statesville (mid $200,000s to mid $800,000s) and Windemere Island in Statesville ($800,000s to the multi-millions).

About Amber Garchar

Amber Garchar is an agent with the Luxury Division of Lake Norman Realty in Cornelius, NC. Her previous experience in marketing, interior design, landscaping and home staging provided an excellent background for her entry into real estate sales in 2007. She lives at the lake, enjoying the many amenities of the area and is knowledgeable on the entire Lake Norman area. She is a licensed broker in North Carolina and helps real estate buyers and sellers in the greater Lake Norman area. She is a member of the national, North Carolina and local Realtors® associations.

Amber has been voted a Five Star Real Estate Agent in Client Satisfaction for five straight years, from 2010 through 2014 by Charlotte Magazine. She is also an Accredited Staging Professional (ASP), a designation awarded to professionals trained in proven home staging techniques.

To learn more about Amber Garchar, visit http://www.amberg.lakenormanrealty.com.

Chapter 5

Chris Bonnefoux

Uptown Charlotte Real Estate

I've been helping buyers and sellers with their Uptown Charlotte real estate needs since 2005. My primary geographic focus is Uptown, within the inner loop, but I also serve some clients in the nearby neighborhoods such as in Dilworth, Myers Park, Elizabeth, Midwood, South End and Midtown as well as in the SouthPark area and with waterfront properties on Lake Norman. Having lived in Uptown condominium buildings since 2003, I am very familiar with Uptown living and have seen all of the Center City growth and changes over the past several years. Over 95% of my clients are condo property buyers or sellers. High-rise condominium buildings have always interested me, as I grew up in a high-rise condo building in New York City. I enjoy all aspects of real estate and the architecture as well as the possibilities for customizations and interior designs. I help clients in the full spectrum of prices, which for Charlotte Uptown condominium buildings generally starts in the $200,000s and run into the millions.

In early 2014 I became the owner of the RE/MAX Exclusive agency here in Uptown Charlotte. I perform some of the marketing and owner duties but my main focus is to be out there working directly with buyers and sellers. This is what I really love to do, helping people with important decisions in their lives. From my first year with RE/MAX, I have ranked in the Top 1% of RE/MAX agents in the Carolinas.

Selling Your Uptown Condo Property

When a condo owner decides to sell their unit, they need to find an agent qualified to market the property and there are many qualifications that a seller should consider. The Uptown condo market is a very specialized one and the first recommendation would be to work with an agent that specializes in condominium complexes. The seller should make inquiries as to the volume of properties the agent has been involved in on both the buying and selling side and make sure that there is a large volume of closed transactions, indicating significant experience. There are some agents that do this as a part-time job, so inquire to make sure the agent is doing this full time, as it is one indicator of the amount of effort that is likely to be put into marketing the property. Having won sales volume awards is another indicator of a successful agent.

Exposure is a major factor in attracting prospective buyers, so make sure the agent describes the marketing plan that will be used to expose the property to the largest number of qualified buyers. There are some agents that may merely "park" the property on the Multiple Listing Service (MLS) and not do much else. That is not likely to result in attracting buyers. Inquire about the advertising and promotion plan that the agent will use.

Past client experiences can also be a good indicator of agent success, so review client testimonials. Uptown Charlotte is a real unique market, so selecting an agent that lives in the Uptown area, and is really in tune with the changes there and has a large network in the area will be another success factor. Finally, sellers will be working with an agent in an important process, so they will want to make sure that the agent they select will be someone they can trust and get along with.

When initially talking with sellers, they generally want advice on market conditions and how to price a property. When it comes to condominiums, some parameters that affect pricing are different from single-family homes. The price will vary depending on several factors including the location, the view, the floor the unit is on, square footage, upgrades and finishes, parking and accessibility. An efficient floor plan will provide more functionality so the value per square foot of a unit can be also vary based on the layout. Sellers should expect the agent to have compelling reasoning behind pricing estimates, factoring in the many variables.

With a condominium property, the seller only has to get the interior updated and ready, as opposed to a single-family home, where sellers have to worry about the entire property. The appearance of the interior is very important. The unit should be warm and inviting, but not overly personalized. When buyers walk through a unit, they need to be able to imagine themselves in the space. An experienced agent can help a seller tailor their space so that it appeals to the widest audience possible.

Sellers generally want to know how long it will take to sell their property. There is not a perfect answer to this, as the time on the market depends on many factors, and really depends on the sellers' preferences. If they are realistic relative to pricing and use the right agent, it will sell quickly. But if waiting for a high price is more important to them, it will take longer to sell. However, I believe strongly in being realistic, and I always tell the client what they can honestly expect to get for their property, so that they're not waiting for something that isn't going to happen and not wasting their time.

Sellers are doing a lot more research before selecting an agent to work with. Some may consider trying to sell the property on their own without an agent. While it's a benefit to be educated as a seller, they should be careful about whether they really want to do it themselves or use a discount broker, just to save more money. While knowledge is power, it's difficult for the typical seller to have the same kind of knowledge and expertise as an experienced realtor. Some sellers have had a difficult experience trying to sell on their own, only to find out it's a completely different and favorable experience once I took on the listing. Sellers are advised to think twice about trying to save money selling a property by themselves, instead of working with a full-time professional.

What Sellers Are Saying:

"Chris was very honest and helpful when listing my condo. He knew exactly what price would move the unit and meet my requirements. Within minutes he also had the repairs and touchups scheduled. A few days and I had an offer in hand!
Chris knows Uptown better than anyone in Charlotte. If you're looking to make moves he is your man! Thank you, Chris!"

"Chris did an absolutely amazing job for my family in selling our condo at 5th and Poplar. He made it a very easy process, handling issues that could have been an aggravation. I highly recommend Chris to anyone I know looking to purchase or sell real estate. He definitely understands customer service, is extremely well connected, and is the best at what he does. I will be using him for future real estate dealings. Thank you Chris!"

Buying Your Uptown Condo Property

The Uptown Charlotte area is the heart of the one of the fastest growing metro areas in the United States and has over 100,000 jobs just within the inner loop. There are dozens of condo buildings, all within walking distance to the many jobs, restaurants, sports and music venues, museums, nightlife and other amenities of Charlotte Center City living.

I ask a lot of questions when starting to work with buyers before beginning to search for specific properties, so I can be sure to show them the best potential buildings for their unique needs. Price range is always the first consideration. I always recommend that buyers make sure to get prequalified for mortgage financing so that they will know for sure what price range they will be able to afford.

Square footage will be one of the most significant factors in the price; but location, view and the package of amenities provided at the building will also be important factors for the price. It is important to understand each buyer's specific set of requirements so we can position them in the most suitable building. Having a short walk to work and maybe a supermarket may be an important factor for some people, while others may be more concerned about the amenities offered in the building where they live. There is a significant range of amenities offered at Uptown condo buildings. There are great buildings that have a pool, fitness center, a concierge (some are even 24 hour), a theater, a clubroom and outdoor grills available. In the end, there is a tradeoff among the unit size, amenities, view and location in the price.

It's important to keep an open mind. Some buyers think that a beautiful city view is their highest priority, only to search a bit and discover that what they actually want is a condo surrounded by trees and gorgeous greenery, and that's okay. I always encourage buyers to remain open to changing their minds throughout the process, because the act of searching can actually be very informative about what it is a buyer thinks is most important.

Homeowners' Associations (HOAs) are an important part of living in a condominium building. The HOA covers the maintenance of all of the amenities, such as pools, landscaping and garages, as well as the exterior and common areas of the property, such as the elevators and hallways. Owners are all jointly responsible for the property upkeep, and owners will pay HOA dues to provide for this on an ongoing basis. While considering various properties, buyers will want to understand the amount of monthly dues required and they should consider that a higher level of amenities to fund in the building will generally require a higher level of HOA dues. This is really a tradeoff with living in a single-family residence, as in such a property the owner directly pays for all maintenance and upkeep. Buyers will want to review the division of responsibilities between themselves and the HOA so there are no surprises down the road.

It is important to also know that HOAs restrict what owners or residents can do with a unit. Buyers should read and understand all the rules and regulations to make sure they're okay with them before buying into a specific building. Restrictions generally apply to such matters as the types of pets allowed and may restrict rental of the property. Some buildings have a cap on the percentage of rentals allowed, so even if the buyer is going to occupy the building initially, at a later date, there may not be the ability to turn their unit into a rental. Another consideration is that the HOA dues are required regardless of the desire to use the amenities, so owners will be paying for the amenities even if they do not need or want the amenities.

In many ways, the due diligence process for buying a condo property is similar to the process for buying a single-family home. The lender will review a condo questionnaire from the building's HOA. This questionnaire will address any issues on the condominium complex as a whole, how many units are rented in the complex, or whether a single owner owns over 10 percent of the units. Buyers should make sure that their lenders do this early in the process to remain on the due diligence timeline.

An inspection will be much simpler than for a single-family house and it will just be assessing the interior of the unit to make sure it's up to par. It is relatively simple, but it is still important so that buyers aren't stuck with a surprise down the road, once they've already closed on the property and moved in.

On a final note, it is important for buyers to find an agent who is experienced enough in the Uptown market to be able to properly match the buyer's requirements with appropriate buildings. Just like for sellers, the buyer should look at client testimonials and should know the agent has significant experience in the Uptown area with a large number of successful closed transactions in the area. Working with an agent that lives in the Uptown area will also be an indicator of one that knows this very local market.

What Buyers Are Saying:

"Due to various reasons my wife and I decided to sell our home and move into an Uptown condo. We evaluated different cities and chose Charlotte, NC. Since we had never lived in Charlotte, we knew no one who could assist us in finding a local Realtor with whom to work. We went online and reviewed different Realtors whom we thought would be a match. We made phone contacts and decided Chris Bonnefoux best suited our personality and had the local market knowledge we were seeking. We have never questioned our decision. He directed us to a condo we ultimately purchased on our very first visit to Charlotte. An excellent Realtor in the truest sense of the word!"

"Chris is the best of the best in Uptown real estate. When our purchase transaction hit a snag that was beyond anyone's control, he was on top of it and made sure everything stayed in motion. When the other broker I chose for my home sale proved to be inexperienced and underwhelming, Chris even went above and beyond and picked up some of her slack – something he should never have had to do. He is an expert negotiator and got us a place we absolutely love. He knows Uptown better than anyone else and is a true expert and professional. Thanks Chris – you really are the very best there is!"

Featured Condo Buildings

The Avenue
The Avenue has 385 units on 36 floors in Uptown's 4th Ward at 210 N. Church Street, two blocks from the square. The building features 1BR, 2BR and penthouse units. Amenities include a 24-hour concierge, a swimming pool on the 10th floor overlooking the city, a large fitness center, a movie theater and a billiards room. Prices range from the $200,000s to over $1 million.

230 South Tryon
The 230 South Tryon Building has 108 units on 13 floors in Uptown's 3rd Ward, two blocks from the square. The building features studios to penthouses. Amenities include a concierge, a swimming pool, a clubroom, a fitness center and a billiards room. Prices range from the $200,000s to in the $ millions.

Trademark
Trademark has 215 units on 28 floors in Uptown's 3rd Ward at 333 West Trade Street, two blocks from the square. The building features studios to penthouses. Amenities include a swimming pool on the 7th floor overlooking the city, a fitness center and outdoor grills. Prices range from close to $200,000 to over $1 million.

Fifth & Poplar
The Fifth & Poplar Building has 304 units on 8 floors in Uptown's 4th Ward at 300 West Fifth Street. The building features studios to penthouses. Amenities include a 24-hour concierge, a fitness center and an approximately 1-acre courtyard with a swimming pool, a putting green and a dog park. Prices range from the upper $100,000s to close to $1 million.

The Ratcliffe
The Ratcliffe Building has 63 units on 9 floors in Uptown's 2nd Ward at 435 South Tryon Street, three blocks from the square. The building features 1BR units to penthouses. The Ratcliffe is overlooking the Green and is the only condo building attached to the over-street mall. The building features ground level retail and dining. There is an historic property tax benefit at this building. Prices range from the $200,000s to over $1 million.

The Trust
The Trust Building has 7 luxury units on 7 floors in Uptown's 2nd Ward at Fourth & Tryon Street, one block from the square. The units range from approximately 3,500 sq. ft. to about 7,000 sq. ft. in half-floor, full-floor and two-story configurations. Amenities include a rooftop terrace and a private entertainment room with billiards. Prices range from the upper $1 millions to over $3 million.

400 North Church
The 400 North Church Building has 83 units on 7 floors in Uptown's 4th Ward. Units range from 2BR to 4 BR. Amenities include a fitness center, a courtyard, secure entry and parking and balconies or patios. Prices range from the $300,000s to over $1 million.

SKYE Condos
The SKYE Condos Building has 69 units on 22 floors in Uptown's 2nd Ward at Third and Caldwell. The building features 1BR units through penthouses. Amenities include a rooftop swimming pool, valet service, a fitness center, a theater room, a game room, a clubroom and a rooftop restaurant. Prices range from the $200,000s to over $2 million.

The Madison
The Madison Building has 26 units on 12 floors in Uptown's 2nd Ward at MLK Boulevard and Caldwell. Units range from 2BR to penthouses. Amenities include a fitness center and

expansive balconies. Prices range from the $400,000s to over $1 million.

Courtside Condos
The Courtside Condos Building has 107 units on 17 floors in Uptown's 1st Ward at 505 E. 6th Street, adjacent to the arena. The building features studios to penthouses. Amenities include secure parking, a waterwall and a rooftop terrace with panoramic city views and a grilling area. Prices range from the $100,000s to the $800,000s.

Settler's Place
Settler's Place has 21 units on 4 floors in Uptown's 4th Ward at 229 N. Church Street, three blocks from the square. This is a historic building with large 2 BR to Penthouse units. There is an historic property tax benefit at this building. Prices range from the $300,000s to over $1 million.

About Chris Bonnefoux

Chris Bonnefoux is the owner of RE/MAX Exclusive in Uptown Charlotte. He is a licensed broker in North Carolina and has been helping real estate buyers and sellers in the Charlotte Uptown/Center City area since 2005. He is an expert in the Uptown condominium market and has lived in four different Uptown condo buildings. He follows his passion for the exciting Center City lifestyle and has used his knowledge of the market to help many hundreds of condo buyers and sellers with their property transactions. He is widely known in the Charlotte real estate community as "Mr. Uptown".

Chris ranks among the top 1% of RE/MAX agents in the Carolinas. RE/MAX is one of the largest real estate agency brands with over 100,000 agents in North America and known for top individual production levels in the industry.

For more information about Chris Bonnefoux and RE/MAX Exclusive, visit http://www.MrUptown.com. He can also be reached at (704) 562-7406.

Chapter 6

Brad Roche

Mortgages

My start in the mortgage industry began in high school when I was an intern in my father's mortgage brokerage business in Michigan. I eventually took over responsibility for the business and along the way have also been involved in a number of related real estate and mortgage industry businesses. In addition to being a mortgage loan officer over the past twenty-one years, I have also been a licensed real estate agent, was lead developer for commercial and residential property developments and was a national mortgage industry sales trainer. We established our presence in the Charlotte area in 2010 and are affiliated with Element Funding.

With two offices in the Charlotte area, one in SouthPark and one in the Lake Norman area, we help borrowers in both North and South Carolina within about two hours from Charlotte. We offer a very broad range of mortgage products for both homebuyers and clients interested in refinancing, including Conventional, FHA, VA, Jumbo loans and others starting in the $200,000s and up into the millions. Every day we get a lot of personal satisfaction in this business knowing that another happy family has been able to purchase their dream home or that a family saved money through refinancing an existing mortgage. We are proud that that vast majority of our business comes from referrals of happy clients.

When looking for a mortgage many people, either interested in purchasing or refinancing a house, focus on the interest rate being advertised, but don't fully consider the cost to acquire the financing. You will see many teaser rates advertised that appear on the surface to be very low interest rates, but what is happening is that there will be a very high closing cost that has to be paid to the get the low rate. Lower is not always better; the best advice is to look at the total cost picture - closing costs as well as monthly payments. When looking for a loan, inquire if loans with no closing costs are available and consider if they may be a good solution for your situation.

The amount of closing costs can be an important consideration for homebuyers. As a buyer, significant cash is required for a down payment and then you have to add in the closing costs. Look at the difference in interest rates and thus monthly payment amounts between a mortgage product with no closing costs compared to one with a lower interest rate, but with significant closing costs. As an example, you may find that the loan with no closing costs will have a monthly payment of $40.00 higher, but the lower rate loan requires $3,000.00 of closing costs. Without taking the time value of money into account it would take about six years of higher monthly payments to equal the out-of-pocket closing costs required. Another thing to consider is how long you will be living in the house and if you will really ever see the break-even point. Younger families, just starting out, are more likely to move within five to seven years as they are growing their families and may want to move to a larger property or relocate due to a job. There may be a different consideration for older couples that plan on retiring in the house and remaining long-term without expectations of moving. Such clients may be more interested in the lower monthly payments for a longer term with not much chance of moving before breaking even. We really like to go over these considerations when starting to work with clients so they gain a good understanding of the tradeoffs involved.

A similar situation applies to clients wanting to refinance as rates reduce. Over the past few years as interest rates were generally declining due to Fed policies, we were able to help many clients refinance their fixed-rate loans, even two or three times, with no financed or out-of-pocket closing costs.

When looking for mortgage financing you may also want to consider the range of mortgage product offerings available to suit your particular needs. A typical large bank will have, let's say, ten different mortgage products available and although they will work for many people, there is not a lot of flexibility. On the other hand, some mortgage bankers, like our firm, offer a much larger range of products. In our case we have over fifty products available, the same ones as the large banks, but many more that may be better suited to the requirements of our clients.

Although we could demonstrate a number of advantages in the flexibility of working with a mortgage provider that offers a wide range of products, let's look at one example. Let's say a homebuyer with good credit and income is looking for a $500,000 loan on a house and wants to keep the down payment at a low level. For houses in our area at this time any loan over $417,000 cannot be done with conventional financing and a "jumbo" loan would be required. Jumbo loans require a higher down payment than conventional loans. One solution we can offer is to get a conventional loan for $417,000 and a second mortgage for the balance. With this solution we maintain the small down payment of the conventional financing and also end up with a great blended interest rate. Some people may call this creativity, but we see this as using our experience and our breadth of loan programs, compared to what will be seen at more typical lenders.

For clients interested in purchasing a house, it is strongly recommended that the buyer get pre-qualified for financing and thus knows the value of a house they can afford. In recent years, sellers are looking for buyers that have already been qualified and many times do not even want their house shown unless there is evidence of pre-qualification. It is important to make sure that the underwriter is experienced and that the pre-qualification will hold, as many times inexperienced mortgage originators do not properly evaluate the borrower's credit capabilities. Our advice would be to ensure that the mortgage originator you are working with can demonstrate several years of experience as well as a good track record in getting a high percentage of pre-qualified loans closed.

The number one complaint in the mortgage industry, year after year, from both clients and realtors, is that they are not kept well informed during the lending process. Make sure to inquire of your mortgage lender how you will be kept updated on the status while your financing is being processed. Several years ago we eliminated this complaint by developing a process where we provide an update every Tuesday by noon to our clients and their agents. Every client gets a Tuesday update in writing so they know exactly where they are at in the lending process.

It's real critical for the buyer to handle all of the contingencies during what is called the "due diligence period" prior to closing a purchase. The buyer puts up a non-refundable deposit and all inspections, appraisal, loan approval and basically anything that can hold up the transaction must be done during this period. Much of this relates to the financing so make sure your lender will get everything on their end completed before the expiration of the due diligence period.

The number two complaint in the industry is that borrowers are surprised at closing with the amount of closing costs. In our initial pre-approval, when they apply online and they are pre-approved, our clients are provided a preliminary closing statement. This is not just an estimate; we give them what is called an HUD-1, which elaborates all of the closing costs to them the day that they apply. It's a closing statement and the client will see the same information at closing. There has generally been improvement in regulations and compliance to limit the surprises at closing; however, we have gone beyond requirements by providing the exact cost information right up front. We also provide a closing package in advance of closing so the client can review all of the documents well in advance. Borrowers see the Note, the Deed, and the Truth In Lending Statement all in advance so that there are no surprises at the closing table.

Although slightly off the topic of mortgages, another piece of advice for buyers or even for someone constructing a new house is to pay attention to the old axiom of not buying the most expensive or largest house in the neighborhood. I recently drove through a new-construction neighborhood with about 40 homes nearing completion. The houses all had brick or stone fronts with siding around the other three sides. This was done to keep the prices in a certain range, and although the houses did not look as good on the sides or the back as the front, that was not such a concern. What I noticed that stood out was one house that had brick on the sides as well as the front. Likely the buyer wanted a better-looking house and chose to upgrade, but that was the only house in the neighborhood with brick on the sides. This probably cost an extra $25,000 for the extra brick in a neighborhood of $300,000 houses, almost a 10% premium. Although the owners may enjoy having brick on the sides of their house, when they decide to sell, they likely will not be able to recover the extra amount paid as they over improved the property, beyond the standard of the neighborhood. When we see clients interested in what appears to be over improving, we are going to advise that they fully recognize the situation and that they are not likely to get the extra money spent back when it comes time to sell a few years away.

What clients are saying:

"Brad, Angela and their team make the loan process easy, efficient and seamless. Highly recommended!"

- Marc M. closed 2014

"Thank you Team Roche! You were able to get my home loan approved when no one else could. We love our home"

- Robert B., closed 2014

"We loved the Tuesday report. It kept us from wondering what was going on!"

- Todd and Heather B., closed 2014

"Brad and his team were incredible to work with. They helped us secure a new home when everyone else said it couldn't be done on our tight budget!"

- Gary and Lisa G., closed 2013, 2014

"This was our third transaction with Brad and I wouldn't hesitate to use him in the future"

- Clint S., closed 2012, 2013, 2014

"This was the easiest and most personable experience I have had with mortgages. Thanks you for making it easy."

- Sharon L., closed 2014

"Brad is one of the most effective and service oriented mortgage bankers you'll ever do business with!"

- Frank A., closed 2012, 2014

Instead of spending a lot of money on advertising and marketing, our philosophy is to give back to our clients with programs that save them money and provides extra benefits that our competitors are not able to offer. A significant amount of our business is from referrals and repeat clients, so we don't have to advertise much for new business. As mentioned before, it is important to provide accurate pre-qualification for our clients to eliminate surprises later in the process. We have chosen to invest in a certified in-house underwriter to assist me in making sure the loans go through properly. This pays off in an extremely high percentage of loans going through without a hitch after the pre-approval.

Like all communities, ours has heroes that put their lives on the line every day like police officers, firemen and military personnel. We have military veterans, many who have risked their lives that we help with VA loans. We also have critical service providers in our community including teachers and medical personnel. We consider all of these people local heroes and we honor them by refunding a percentage of their closing costs when they obtain financing though us.

When we moved from Michigan and established our first office in Charlotte, the country was in the middle of a major recession and we started building relationships in the community with local businesses that even years later are providing benefits to our clients. We initially offered to save these businesses' employees money on their closing costs by being their preferred lender and the businesses reciprocated with benefits for all of our clients - savings on their products and services. Our clients get an electronic package every quarter with various savings from our business partners. This benefits our business partners' employees as well as our clients.

Relocations are always stressful and we try to minimize the stress for relocating clients as much as possible. We've been licensed as a travel planners so we can arrange flights, hotels and auto rentals to make is easier for house-hunting trips to the area and to pass on the savings to the clients, not to make a profit for us. We can even arrange dinner reservations for them.

We started our local business relationships with the Human Resources Managers of our business partners where we were the preferred lenders. This led to another opportunity we can

85

provide for relocating families. Frequently when someone relocates to the Charlotte area, the spouse needs to find a job in the local area as well. We use our connections with our many businesses partners to take the spouse's resumes and promote employment with these businesses. This is another way we do as much as we can to bring as much savings, as much benefit to make relocating clients' lives easier. All of these extra benefits have grown over the years into what we call our "Passport to Charlotte".

What associates and partners are saying:

"We appreciate the consistent professionalism and efficiency demonstrated by you and your office. The clients are always happy and well informed which makes the closing process so much less stressful for everyone involved. Keep up the great work."

- Ben Thomas, Attorney at Law, Thomas and Godley Attorneys

"When you need someone to clarify the options out there and get the job done and done right, Brad Roche is who we have our clients call."

- Jeffrey Carbone, CFP, Cornerstone Financial Partners, Inc.

"Brad is a great resource for all of your mortgage needs. Brad gets the best program for the customer and has their interest in mind. He makes everything easy with First Class service and communications that are second to none."

- Howard Culbreth, Insurance Agent, State Farm Insurance

"The clients I have sent to Brad have appreciated his service and attention to detail. With his years of experience, his knowledge allows his customers to know that they will get

all their questions answered and be comfortable with the process."

- Keith Taylor, ChFC, CLU, Financial Strategist, Centerpoint Associates

"Brad's team goes above and beyond for a smooth closing, and they always close on time"

- Rene Poteat, Sales Associate, Meritage Builders

About Brad Roche

Brad Roche is known among the Charlotte area real estate industry as "The Mortgage Planner". He has been a mortgage loan officer for over twenty-one years and consistently ranks in the Top 1% in the United States for loan originations, closing over 200 loans per year. He is affiliated with Element Funding and manages four offices in the Carolinas, including three in the Charlotte area. He also has a weekly radio show that is broadcast in North and South Carolina by four stations including CBS, Fox and ESPN.

Brad's experience along with mortgage lending also includes eleven years as a licensed real estate agent, nine years as a national mortgage sales trainer and lead developer on multi-million dollar commercial and residential projects. He has been a Direct Endorsed Underwriter for HUD for ten years and has several certifications in leadership training. Additionally he is a certified class instructor with Central Piedmont Community College, the largest community college in the nation.

For more information about Brad Roche, visit

http://www.TheMortgagePlanner.net.

Chapter 7

Lisa Archer

Buying and Selling Charlotte Residential Real Estate

I started in the real estate business in Charlotte in 2005 after working in sales and branch management in the banking industry. I saw a good opportunity to use my sales abilities in this dynamic real estate market here in Charlotte, so I decided to leave the banking industry and initially started working in real estate with my father. Seeing the rapid change in technology being used for real estate sales, the growth of the Charlotte region and the need to be able to offer a higher level of services to my clients, I decided to form the Live Love Homes Team at Keller Williams.

At Live Love Homes we have about fifteen team members here in our Charlotte hub and we are establishing expansion teams in other markets in the United States under our umbrella. Our local team includes specialists for key functions in the buying and selling process. We have property listings specialists, a marketing manager, buyer's agents, a specialist that works with veterans and other local heroes, an international specialist that works with our international relocation clients and an administrative team. This way our clients get the benefit of working with an expert for their particular needs instead of relying on one agent to handle everything.

Our team helps buyers and sellers in the entire Charlotte area, within about an hour of Charlotte. Our agents live throughout the area as well so we are very familiar with the entire region. We help clients in all price ranges from starter houses and lots up to the multi-million dollar luxury homes. We also help investors find and close profitable investment properties in the area.

Selling Your Charlotte Area Home

When a seller initially contacts us, the first question is generally related to how much their house is worth; what it will sell for. To provide the most help we need to know a little about their situation. We want to know what is motivating the sale, when they are moving, where they are moving to and do they already know if they will be able to purchase where they are moving. We make sure they have looked at their credit report and have been at least pre-qualified by a lender so they are pretty sure that they will be able to purchase another house. We want to eliminate as much as possible of the uncertainty, because if they put their house on the market and we receive an offer, and then the seller can't buy or close on a new purchase, the seller has a problem.

It's important that a seller talk to a professional agent as soon as they have determined that they are going to be moving or selling. Often the property needs some repairs or upgrades and talking with a professional in advance can save money. Most homeowners aren't able to determine what should actually be done to the property to maximize value, given the neighborhood and what is owed on the property, and we want to make sure they don't overspend. There's nothing worse than spending too much to renovate a house to the point where it's gone beyond neighborhood standards and there is no way to get the investment back upon sale. We have a contractor we refer our clients to that specializes in prepping properties for sale and they make sure the clients don't overspend.

After understanding the seller's situation and if any repairs are needed, we go to work establishing the suggested listing price for the property. We pull comparable sales data over the past three months if there are enough sales; if not, we go back six months. We also gather photos of the sold properties so the sellers can see the condition of the properties and be able to rate them. Armed with this information, we sit with the seller and work out the listing price based on facts. It's important to work with an agent that will provide enough comparable sales data to be able to know that the decision will based on actual numbers and actual homes that have been sold. In this way sellers will be more knowledgeable on realistic pricing and will be better able to leave emotion out of the decision.

An important pricing factor in today's market is the manner in which houses are marketed online. Most buyers are looking online for houses so the pricing strategy needs to reflect that reality. In the past a house valued at around $200,000 might be listed at $198,000, as it was believed that just under $200,000 would attract more buyers. In today's Internet environment, houses are classified by range so buyers can select a range to search. In this example the price point ranges might be $150,000 to $200,000 and $200,000 to $250,000. In such a case where a property value is just near the range break point, the appropriate price for listing would be $200,000 as buyers looking in both price ranges would then see this listing, possibly doubling the exposure to potential buyers.

Some sellers make the mistake of trying to get their house listed at well above the estimated market value, as they may believe that the higher price allows for room to negotiate with potential buyers, and they can always reduce the price if they aren't receiving any offers. This is really a mistake and the result is like chasing a ball down a hill and you're never going to catch it. If you start overpriced, by the time you start dropping the price, people see that the property has been listed for a long time and that you're dropping it in small amounts. It's going to be very hard to catch up and you're going to end up selling it for less than if it had been priced properly at the beginning. When people see a house that's been on the market for a while they want to low ball because they think something's wrong with it. When they look at the listing history, they see it 's been at several different prices. Then they know it started out overpriced and now believe the seller is desperate and they're going to make a lower offer than they would have otherwise. Perception is reality, whether it's true or not.

I talked earlier about proper pricing positioning for online searches. With property exposure moving so rapidly to the Internet, sellers should inquire of their agent how their property will be marketed online. Syndicating your listing to sites like Trulia and Zillow and other online portals is important and not all agents do this. Properties not showing up on these sites could take longer to sell and may not sell for as much. This brings up another point regarding safety and security. Sellers should make sure to approve all photos that are going to be used in online marketing. You don't want your children or any photos of your children that may be on the walls to be in photos that are going to be used in any online marketing. Your address is going to be online when you're selling your home, so you just want to make sure that you are safeguarding your family.

We recommend insisting to your agent that only pre-approved buyers are shown the house. As a seller, you don't want to spend a lot of time cleaning up the house for a showing and then find out later that the buyer looking at your house was interested, but unfortunately was not approved for a loan that would qualify to purchase the house.

One benefit of working with a Realtor team like Live Love Homes is the breadth of expertise within our team. Instead of working with one agent we have specialists handling each part of the listing and marketing process. As an example we have one team member, the listing manager, who sets up the listing, orders the professional photographs and selects the ones to showcase the property. She also organizes the property listing on all of the syndicated online sites. Another team member focuses on marketing the properties. She organizes promotions for all of our listed properties like open houses for other agents and potential buyers. She plans media advertising for our listings and decides if the type of property would benefit from a virtual video tour. We also proactively market our listings to our buyer database where we have interested buyers classified by price range and location.

When selling your house the main contributors are pricing it properly, the location, the condition and exposure to potential buyers. The location is a given that can't be controlled, but the seller can control the condition and the price. Make sure to select an agent that has the experience and provides a rational documentation of the property value and demonstrates a marketing plan that will expose the property to the highest number of potential buyers, including a comprehensive Internet presence.

What Sellers Are Saying:

"Live Love Homes is amazing. We had a really difficult closing and Live Love Homes was fantastic to work with because the company is great at negotiations and really goes the extra mile"

"Live Love Homes set the bar very high in selling my home and made me feel important and put my needs first."

Buying Your Charlotte Area Home

When we first start to work with buyers we want to understand their wants and needs. We have a buyer questionnaire and we interview them to gather most of the information we need to be able to properly assist them. We need to make sure we know their requirements such a location parameters, size of house, number of bedrooms, special location requirements, such as near to a hospital, desired proximity to shopping, size of yard desired, need for a fenced yard for a dog, and so on. We also want to find out the expected price range and if they are already approved for a loan. Most sellers only want their properties shown to pre-approved buyers and will not accept offers unless the buyer is approved, so this is an important early step for any buyer.

Most local move-up buyers know the area and have a pretty good idea of the general locations that would work for them. As a rapidly growing metro area, the Charlotte region attracts many business relocations and individual transfers and we are geared up to help relocation buyers find their ideal home in the region. One of the common criteria for out-of-area buyers will be the proximity of the home to the office or workplace and possibly the airport. They know where they will be working but they need to know what the commute is going to be like, to and from various areas that they will be considering. We like to drive them around to several areas during the first day of a house hunting trip so they can get a good feel of the community and get a sense of some areas where they will be interested in a more detailed look. We then suggest they check the commute traffic in real time by making a trip from the employment location to the potential living area at about 5:00 pm or from the opposite direction during the morning commute hours. If commuting times are a concern, it is better to understand the reality upfront instead of hating a hard commute after buying a property.

After the buyer has selected a property and we negotiate the price and terms on their behalf and an offer is accepted, we work with the buyer to complete due diligence on the property. We provide a list of recommended licensed inspectors, attorneys and other vendors. A full mechanical and structural inspection should always be completed and this will also include a termite inspection. Although radon is not a common issue in this region, there are some specific areas where the inspector will perform a radon test due to a higher potential for risk. Many neighborhoods, especially outside city limits aren't on city water and sewer services; in such cases, a well water test and septic system inspection are recommended. If there is a swimming pool at the property, the pool and equipment should be inspected. We also recommend that buyers consider home warranties and we refer them to available options.

We enjoy working with first-time homebuyers and we even have a specialist on our team that works with them. Just like with most things, when people are doing something for the first time, like buying a house, they may need more help and advice. First-time homebuyers should look for an agent that will have the patience to answer all of their questions, will walk them through the complete process and show where to find the information they need. They may need advice in interpreting the various documents and inspection reports and the agent should be willing to help.

What Buyers Are Saying:

"Live Love Homes went above and beyond my expectations and I would recommend them to everyone I know. My agent listened to my wish list I had for a house and nailed it by finding a house that had everything I wanted and more that was within my price range. It was a pleasure to work with Live Love Homes and made the entire experience as simple and as easy on me as possible. You won't go wrong with Live Love Homes."

"As a young female buying my first home in an area I knew nothing about, Live Love Homes was willing to answer all my questions and put forth the extra effort to help me understand the ins and outs of buying a home. I dreaded the home-buying process when I first started, but as soon as I started working with my agent, she made sure it was as effortless on my end as possible. I will forever be grateful for Live Love Homes!"

Homes for Heroes® Program

Live Love Homes participates in a unique program that provides substantial savings for our local heroes. With our affiliation with Homes for Heroes we are able to provide a 25% rebate of our commission to heroes who work with us to buy or sell their house. The Homes for Heroes program was established after the tragic events of 9/11 to provide savings and rewards to local heroes who provide necessary and important services to our communities every day. Heroes eligible for this program include firefighters, police officers, teachers, health care workers, emergency responders and active and retired military personnel. Buyers or sellers that qualify as a hero should contact Love Live Homes so they can get enrolled in the program and be eligible for the substantial savings offered.

About Lisa Archer

Lisa Archer is COO of Live Love Homes with Keller Williams in Charlotte. She is a licensed broker in both North Carolina and South Carolina and is a Certified Military Residential Specialist (CMRS). She has been in the forefront of online real estate marketing and is a trainer and speaker on real estate Internet marketing, social media and technology. Live Love Homes is currently expanding into eight additional markets around the United States.

Lisa was named as one of the Inman News 100 Most Influential in Real Estate in 2013 and 2014. She was also listed as one of the Swanepoel Power 200 and sits in Gary Keller's Top 100 Mastermind Group.

For more information on Lisa Archer and Live Love Homes, visit
http://LiveLoveHomes.com.

Chapter 8

Darin Brockelbank

Outdoor Living Spaces

My entrepreneurial life began at age fourteen after my family moved to Charlotte and I started Darin's Lawn Care to earn some spending money. Over a few years, while still a teenager, I had a real interest in everything about landscaping and I started to see what was becoming a trend in California and parts of Florida that has evolved into what is now being called "Outdoor Living". At age nineteen, I started college but decided that I wanted to build an entire company around the trend of outdoor living, which would include hardscaping for patios and walks, outdoor fireplaces and kitchens, fire pits, gazebos and other structures, swimming pools and other landscaping features. Metro GreenScape was born and we started to educate the marketplace here in the Charlotte area just before the national phenomenon around outdoor living began. Charlotte is a great area for outdoor living as we have a moderate four-season climate and most outdoor living features can be used at least nine months of the year.

Metro GreenScape has evolved and developed since our founding into an award winning company that designs and builds all ranges of residential outdoor living and landscape projects as well as maintains landscaping. Our maintenance division performs basic lawn care and full landscaping maintenance in the immediate Charlotte/Mecklenburg area, including the adjacent suburbs. Our focus is on residential maintenance but we also handle some commercial properties as well. Our light construction division handles semi-custom outdoor construction where clients want a high quality job with local products. This division has a larger coverage area including all of Charlotte/Mecklenburg County and also ranging from the northern part of Lake Norman through eastern Gaston County, the Lake Wylie area including northern York County, to Waxhaw and northwestern Union County to the eastern Charlotte suburbs adjoining Mecklenburg County.

Our custom division focuses on larger projects, generally over $100,000 and where the clients can customize the selection of design features and materials. This division covers a much larger area, from the beach to the mountains. Many of our Charlotte area clients have a second home at the beach, a lake, in the mountains or in the country and they are interested in having us handle the design and outdoor construction for their other home as well. When we do a project in these areas many times we are referred to other homeowners in the same area.

We have a philosophy here at Metro GreenScape we call, "Changing lives, impacting people". We apply this philosophy internally within the company as well as with clients and in giving back to the community. We apply this internally by mentoring the individuals on our team and helping them grow to the next level, creating new opportunities for our company. For our clients we do everything so that they are served and don't have to stress or worry about something while a project is underway. We change the way they entertain in their yard and many times they form additional relationships with people that might not have formed as a result of us creating a space where they can entertain, have people over and spend more time with children and grandchildren.

It's not about our product or the service. It's more about relieving stress for people so they can come home and relax and have a mini vacation in their yard with the people they choose to spend their time with. Some of our clients are athletes or executives and they're on the road all the time. It's a way to relax when they come home. Others, like doctors, have very stressful jobs and they may want to dip in the pool and unwind after a tough day. Some people may be retired and want a nice patio or courtyard and maybe a wall fountain where they can go out and read the paper, watch the butterflies and relax. Some want to get to know their neighbors and spend time relaxing outdoors. Maybe it's just a patio and a fire pit. It doesn't matter the size of the project. At the end of the day, we're impacting people and changing lives in a positive manner.

When a consumer first contacts us we ask a lot of questions to make sure we understand generally what they are looking for and if we will be a good fit for their project. We try to determine what their pain points are, what their needs are and if we have solutions that will fit their requirements. We also try to understand which of our staff is the best match to work with the prospective client. It could be based on project scale or even the personality of the consumer. We have a sales/service business model where the same person works with the consumer from the initial meeting or consultation, through the estimating, the design, the product selections, purchasing, project management and at the end to close out the project and make sure the client is happy with the result.

Much of the time consumers may not know precisely what they want and are not familiar with project costs so we offer a seventy-five dollar consultation. We don't try to sell anything when we do a consultation, because we are only giving advice. We will consider the consumer's budget and provide estimating guidelines on the cost of various features and even help the consumer prioritize their wants and needs to match their budget.

If the consumer wants to go to the next step, we offer a range of design services depending on the level of detail the consumer needs. Some people can visualize really well so they may not need as much detail; but others need to see things in 3D, so we can provide that if desired. Of course the cost of the design work increases with the complexity. Our design process is very collaborative with the consumer. They may have photos and we generally visit completed projects we have done so they can see a range of features and options. We will also visit materials suppliers so they can get a better understanding of colors and textures available. When the design is completed we will work with the consumer to best work out the project within the allotted budget and we have access to financing, if that is needed. Just because we have done the design, we don't assume that we automatically will do the construction. Once we have completed the design with specifications, the consumer can decide to work with us for full implementation or they can take it to other contractors to bid out, if they desire.

Outdoor living spaces and improvements are for a lifestyle enhancement but homeowners should be knowledgeable about the potential value on resale. Getting all of your information from the home improvement reality-style television shows and the Internet is not the best approach, as resale value of improvements is often inflated. We've had a lot of discussions with appraisers in the area and we have a pretty good idea of the improvements that are going to give money back at resale. While some improvements bring a good return, others will not, and some improvements just get the property up to the standard in the neighborhood.

There are some rules-of-thumb we use to evaluate the maximum amount of outdoor improvement value on a property that will likely be recovered in a resale. As the property value in the type of neighborhood rises, the standard of outdoor improvement expectation rises as well. For a starter home about one percent of the value of the home is the maximum. As you move to a mid-priced home, which in the Charlotte area is between $200,000 and $400,000, the expectation is three to four percent of the home value. For a higher value neighborhood in the $500,000 to $800,000 range, five to seven percent would be the standard. When you consider luxury homes in the million dollar and over range, about ten percent of the value would be the most you would want to invest to get the investment back.

The type of improvement influences the return of investment at resale. Anytime you put a roof over an area, such as a patio, you are adding unheated square footage and appraisers generally will provide a value based on the added unheated square footage. There is more value returned for improvements where there is a popular trend, such as in outdoor living spaces – patios, outdoor kitchens, fire pits and fireplaces. If you're looking at making your turf better or putting in something for privacy, that's really more of an emotional purchase and may not bring any return.

For larger projects, some homeowners consider phasing the project out to conserve cash. One point to consider is that phasing the project normally adds about fifteen percent to the total cost of the project because there are multiple delivery fees, tractor drop-offs and materials may cost a bit more as there may be less opportunity for bulk purchase discounts. A project that would cost $100,000 if done at one time, but split into three phases over time, would likely cost about $115,000. Homeowners should compare that cost to the cost of financing all or part of the project, and compare the interest cost for the period of the financing. Of course, if adding more debt, homeowners should make sure that income will be secure and not likely to be threatened, so that additional financing payments can be made.

Most of the time homeowners don't ask the right questions of their outdoor living or landscaping contractor. The most reliable companies want you to do your homework and ask the really tough questions, as they don't have anything to hide. If the contractor has a fairly quick and good answer that can be validated, the chances are that they have integrity. With most projects, the homeowner and contractor will be working together for a while so personal compatibility will be important. This usually can be determined during the initial discussions and the manner in which the contractor answers difficult questions, which the homeowner should be asking.

Homeowners should always ask about insurance – Workmen's Compensation and General Liability. They should ask to see the Certificate of Insurance for proof. We rarely get asked to see the insurance certificate and lack of proper contractor's insurance is one of the largest risk factors for homeowners if something goes wrong, such as an injury to a worker or damage to the property or to a neighbor's property caused by the contractor. Make sure that insurance information provided by a contractor is backed up with proof.

Rarely do we hear homeowners asking about permitting and the contractor's record with permits. They just assume the contractor is doing the right thing. Most of the outdoor construction projects we do require a building permit, yet at least 60% of the contractors working don't get a permit. Make sure the contractor is going to get all required permits and also ask about their permitting record, such as what percentage of the time their work passes the first inspection. Homeowners should validate this information by making an inquiry with the local permitting agency.

Every contractor, even the best, has had some bad experiences with their customers; the difference is how they are handled. A valid question to ask is about the contractor's last bad experience with a client and how it was handled. Look at the Better Business Bureau ratings, the number of complaints and how the complaints were resolved. If the contractor denies any bad experiences, it is not likely to be true as any contractor that has been in business for a while has had something go wrong on a project.

Rarely are we ever asked about how we handle the warranty. We would encourage homeowners to ask about the warranty policy and to also ask for some examples of when the warranty had to be honored. Request to talk to prior customers who had issues and the warranty had to be honored and ask what the experience was like.

We recommend inquiring if the contractor is a member of a local homebuilders or remodeling company association. These associations have strong ethical and legal standards that all members must meet to become members. Many of these associations also have annual competitions for best project awards where a committee of peer companies votes on the best completed projects. A good indicator of a competent contractor is one that has won a number of such awards.

If homeowners ask the right questions and the answers and verifications appear to check out, the chances of success are greater and you will likely be dealing with a company with integrity. By working with a company that has integrity and is a one-stop turnkey solution, you will avoid the bait-and-switch, the multiple change orders with higher costs and you will decrease the finger pointing between contractors that oftentimes leads to one of them not taking responsibility, where at the end, the consumer has to pay more out of pocket.

Metro GreenScape has maintenance programs for lawn care as well as comprehensive landscape maintenance services, including flowerbed maintenance, plant and flower fertilization, plant disease control and irrigation and outdoor lighting system maintenance. While lawn care appears to be a simple commodity service, there are some important questions homeowners should be asking to make sure they select the right lawn care and maintenance company. Surprisingly, homeowners will find very few lawn care service companies will be able to properly answer the questions. The first important question to ask is how they avoid transfer of weed and Bermuda grass seeds between lawns that they are cutting. This is important because a mower can have millions of weed seeds in the deck after cutting a lawn. The correct answer is to thoroughly clean the mower after cutting each lawn and before moving it to another yard. This takes as much as ten minutes and few lawn care companies do this. Another question to ask is what height the mowers are set to cut the lawn. If they don't answer that it depends upon the season of the year and that they adjust the cutting height to match the proper height for the grass condition, depending on the season, they are not going to be leaving your lawn in a healthy condition. Also you should ask how the company will be looking out for signs of issues, such as a fungus or other turf diseases, in advance, so that preventive measures can be taken.

What Clients Are Saying

"I really appreciated your efforts. Since our initial meeting, it has been a pleasure working with you and your company. After working with numerous contractors through the past few years, I have experienced inconsistent results. Your professionalism, consistency, quality and timeliness helped me regain my confidence towards contractors. The patio met all of our expectations. It is absolutely gorgeous. From me and my family, thank you for the excellent work!"

- Andrew P.

"We recently built a new home and our lot was an undeveloped, wooded lot. Metro GreenScape, Inc. transformed the lot to a well-manicured, beautifully landscaped yard with green grass and natural area, while maintaining the natural trees all around. It was amazing to watch the transformation in only a few short days. We couldn't be more satisfied with the result. WHAT A HUGE DIFFERENCE! Darin and Heather really know their business. Every detail of the landscaping process was explained, so that we would know exactly what we were getting. Dealing with them was a real pleasure. Not only are they knowledgeable about landscaping, they are also punctual and very reasonably priced. The finished product was even better than we had expected."

- Rick B.

"I wanted to say thank you for the great work that you and your team did for me. My yard looks great now thanks to Metro GreenScape. I would also like to say thank you for going that extra mile by replacing some parts of the sod that didn't take root properly during the initial installation. Thank you very much for your time and commitment to excellence. I have already recommended you to several people who are looking to have landscaping and sod renovations.

Best of luck in the future. God Bless!"

- John H.

"I would like to thank Metro GreenScape, Inc. for an outstanding job on the installation of my new patio. You and your team have turned my patio dream into reality; the design and colors match perfectly the natural landscape of my back yard. Again, thank you for your wisdom and vision in exceeding all my expectations."

-Bernard M.

About Darin Brockelbank

Darin Brockelbank is the Founder, President and Chief Visionary Officer of Metro GreenScape, Inc. based in Charlotte, NC. As an entrepreneur at a young age, he started and then built Metro GreenScape into one of the Carolinas' leading and award winning comprehensive turnkey outdoor living and landscaping design/build and maintenance companies.

Metro GreenScape delivers a wide range of design/build outdoor living projects including custom design/build projects. The company is expanding its coverage range and the future scope will include from the coast to the mountains. Projects include patio and walk hardscapes, swimming pools, outdoor fireplaces, fire pits, outdoor kitchens, pergolas, gazebos and traditional landscaping. Metro GreenScape also has a landscape maintenance division that not only performs lawn service but also full landscape maintenance in the greater Charlotte Metro area.

As a local small business leader, Darin has won a number of awards including NARI Contractor of the Year, Best of Show Award in 2013; Lake Norman Home Builders Association Best of the Lake, First Place for Landscaping Project $50,000 and above in 2014; and Top 12 Finalist for National Landscaper of the Year in 2012.

Metro GreenScape is a member of NARI, the National Association of Remodelers Industry, the Lake Norman Homebuilders Association and is an Accredited Company with the Charlotte Better Business Bureau.

For more information about Darin Brockelbank and Metro GreenScape, visit http://www.metrogreenscape.com or visit the company Facebook page at https://www.facebook.com/MGScharlotte?ref=br_rs. The company can be reached by telephone at (704) 839-2620.

Chapter 9

Linda Beverley and Leslie J. Dale

Investment Properties

We are both affiliated with RE/MAX Executive in Charlotte. We often work as a team when assisting real estate investors, because the pace is so fast in the investment market. Our investment clients are local, from different areas of the country and a number are from Asia, Europe and South America. Both of us enjoy helping investors in making profitable decisions and we love introducing all that Charlotte has to offer to new clients.

Buying rental properties is easy. There are countless books, television shows and seminars readily available that tell you how to do so in 5 – 10 easy steps.

However... MAKING A GOOD INVESTMENT in Real Estate is not at all easy.

Real Estate Investing is a real business and it has to be conducted as such. It is not without risk and the research on each deal must be done carefully to make sure there is an excellent profit and return on investment. Finding a good team who has experience with investment properties in the local market will remove most of the risk and help you on the path to profitable investing.

Charlotte has received a lot of attention in the national press about favorable conditions for real estate investment. The region has been among the fastest growing metro areas in the country for many years, fueled by a great business climate, moderate cost of living and corporate relocations to the area. A number of Wall Street institutional investors have set up investment funds with a focus on single family homes in the Charlotte area. There are also countless investors from abroad actively investing in the region. So don't think you're going to get a "steal" on every deal in and around Charlotte. Remember, the sellers are reading this same information. What we do offer our clients are good solid investments with low risks and a better than average chance at excellent appreciation rates.

Some clients want to purchase and quickly flip properties. Others want to develop a portfolio of rental properties to hold. Most pursue a combination of both. Regardless of the direction you want to take, local knowledge and expertise is key to being successful. Investors should assemble a team of specialists to work with them through this process. This includes an excellent real estate attorney, at least two solid lenders who know their product lines and an excellent Realtor with extensive local knowledge and experience, who can find suitable investments at all levels.

Competition is fierce for the most attractive investment properties. It's crucial to have an experienced team who will

1. rapidly identify the properties to evaluate
2. estimate any repairs, updates or renovations needed
3. work the numbers and
4. determine whether the property is a potentially good investment or not.

Inspectors are needed to check out the mechanical, plumbing and electrical systems and the structure. Rehab work is almost always required, especially for flip projects, so an investor will need contractors that can quickly complete the rehab work in an economical and timely manner. Many investors we work with are not in our local area. Depending on the project, we may hire a project manager to visit the property every day to ensure that the project stays on time and on budget.

The first step, of course, is to locate suitable investment properties. We are constantly "house hunting", touring and evaluating properties that appear to meet basic criteria that we have established.

The most important step is to "Do the Math". As an example, let's assume we find a property in a neighborhood where we can expect a retail price of $125,000 for a house in good shape. Once you determine the retail selling price, work backwards to determine the maximum investment purchase price. For a target selling price of $125,000 we would advise a target profit of at least $20,000.

We generally figure 10% of the reconditioned retail value for the investor's transaction costs on both the buying and selling end and for taxes and insurance during the short holding period. In this case, that would be $12,500. From the age and the conditions we observe at the property, we have a very good idea of what the rehab costs will be. For the property we are considering, let's estimate $35,000. We need to consider a rehab project manager fee into the rehab cost, unless the investor is local and will be personally managing the work. Estimate the project manager cost at 10% of the rehab cost, in this case $3,500. Subtract these from the maximum retail selling price to determine the maximum purchase price of this investment property. This is determined from the expected sale price of $125,000 and subtracting the expected profit and the costs. We are left with a maximum purchase price of $54,000. An offer like this may insult the sellers; however, this is an example for an older house in a middle-class neighborhood, which has not been updated and needs a lot of work. Other knowledgeable buyers will have a similar viewpoint about needed repairs. In a case like this, a price of about $54,000 would be the most an investor should pay to guarantee the expected return, based on the condition and the location. The hard part is convincing the sellers.

Good candidates for flip properties are purchased rapidly. It is important to immediately detect properties coming to market, and to know the numbers in order to make an offer within a day or two, or someone else will buy the property. Inspections are crucial, but rather than to obtain a general inspection, we more often utilize specialists for critical systems such as structure, HVAC, plumbing, electrical and termites.

Due to the high level of rehab activity in the area, contractors are very busy, so it's important to schedule the repair work as soon as an offer is accepted. We work to coordinate the purchase closing with the contractors' availability, to minimize the holding time. Depending on the amount of work needed, investors should expect that one to three months will be required to rehab the property and get it ready to market. The average amount of time that properties are on the market varies with the time of year and the overall market situation. As we are writing this, the Charlotte market is well balanced, and the average time on market is in the range of 80 days. A pretty house that has been properly repaired and is priced right will sell quickly.

Many investors are looking for a long-term passive income with higher return on investment compared to other alternatives, or they want to diversify their investments. Rental properties can be an attractive investment vehicle for such investors. Just as with investing in short-term flip properties, purchasing rental properties requires "Doing the Math". Otherwise, the investor may get stuck with an investment that is not making a return. We frequently see new investors getting an emotional attachment to a property. They may see a nice property that is very attractive and think they would like to purchase the house as an investment. Just like with flip properties, they really need to look carefully at the numbers and make sure there will be a reasonable rate of return. Much of the time the nicest house doesn't make the best investment.

When analyzing a potential rental property, the investor needs to consider the upfront investment cost, which includes the purchase price, the buyer's closing costs, and the cost of repairs or renovations that are needed. Sometimes there are systems that don't have that much useful life left, but don't need immediate replacement. In such a case, the investor, who will be the landlord, is advised to include the cost of replacement in the repair costs, as such an expense will likely be required in the near term.

We research the expected rental income and the ongoing estimated expenses to determine the net rental income. The ongoing expenses include property taxes, insurance, a provision for vacancy, and a provision for maintenance and property management fees. We generally use one month's rent in a year as a vacancy factor, and also as an estimate of maintenance expenses. With this information, the investor can calculate the estimated yield on the property, before and after mortgage payments. Just like with a property that is going to be flipped, the investor can work backwards and calculate the maximum purchase price for the property that will achieve the desired yield and return on investment. It's critical to get the numbers right, because if they are off substantially, what may on the surface look attractive, could turn out to be a poor investment and could result in a negative cash flow, costing money every month. Working with an experienced Realtor in rental properties is an important factor for success.

Most of the time, an investor will make a higher return on investment with a number of smaller rental properties than one larger single-family rental property. This is because the rental revenue doesn't go up proportionally with the property value. Although this is the normal case, each individual deal needs to be analyzed and "Doing the Math" will provide the answer.

Another important point is that some properties will make a good profit in a flip, while others might be more suitable for long-term holding for rental. Again, each deal is different and investors have to run the numbers to determine if a property will bring a suitable return. We advise our clients to work with an accountant very familiar with real estate investing to optimize the tax treatment for income producing properties. Certain decisions, such as allocation of the value between land and improvements, need to be made upfront, and a good accountant can provide the best advice in this area.

When entering the real estate investment business, either for the first time or in a new area, investors should be careful to choose an agent to work with that has a lot of experience with investment properties. It's quite a bit different than looking for a place to make your home. Experience in locating suitable investments, knowledge about repair and rehabilitation, and the economics of good deals are imperative. A significant amount of our activity is directed toward investment properties. We daily check on new listings, and quickly make an assessment of the investment potential so we can notify our clients of possible deals. As mentioned earlier, the best investment property deals need to be acted upon rapidly or they will be sold before the typical agent is even aware of them. Anyone can help purchase a property, but it is important to find an agent you can trust to make sure that you are going to make a good investment decision.

Rental property investors will also need to consider how to manage their properties. Out-of-area investors absolutely need to have their properties locally managed. Local investors may think they want to manage the properties on their own, but that's rarely a good idea. It's much better to have a "buffer" between the tenants and landlords. It allows you to leave emotions out and make sound business decisions.

Typical property management duties include

1. advising on the appropriate rental rate
2. keeping the property rented by finding and screening qualified tenants
3. handling tenant complaints and
4. overseeing repairs and maintenance.

Investors will want to work with a property manager that is looking out for the investor's best interest and has experience managing for investors in the local market.

We handle property management for most of our rental property investor clients; some will not buy unless we agree to manage for them. We are very hands-on and do some things differently than other management firms. Tenant quality is the foundation of a good experience owning rental properties. We don't just put up a for lease sign. We list the property for rent through the Multiple Listing Service, or MLS, as we find the best quality tenants come through a Realtor, and people working with a Realtor are more likely to be homeowners at heart. When we are asked to manage a property, one of the first things we do is to introduce ourselves to the neighbors. We give them our card and let them know they can call us if there is any trouble. We handle all of the calls from tenants and the repairs and maintenance for the property. Our objective is to make the owning experience very stress-free for the rental property investor.

Most people buying rental properties buy the cheapest property they can find. Those houses are cheap for a reason. Sellers have learned to hide a lot of damage with new paint and carpet. That lovely new tile board surrounding the bathtub/shower may push in because the wall behind it is totally rotted. The tenant calls because the toilet is loose and rocky and during the repairs you find the floor underneath must be replaced. And it's not just the subfloor, but also the floor joists and sill beams as well. The house may have new replacement windows, but they didn't replace the frames, so water is penetrating into the walls and rotting the wood from the inside. You checked the heating and air units, but did you

119

inspect the ductwork? The house has air conditioning so you think the wiring is up to date. Guess again.

You make a good return renting the homes in the beginning, and then the problems begin. Now the properties are "eating money" and you decide to sell them. Unfortunately, they aren't worth what you paid for them and you can't find a buyer. Finally you decide to find a real estate agent experienced in investment properties.
... Not a month goes by that we don't get a call to try to get someone out of a mess. We can help, but there is no magic pill.

Many of the television programs on real estate investing focus on "flipping" houses where the investor is looking to find a distressed property, purchase and rehab it quickly, then resell for a healthy profit.

With all of the publicly advertised seminars, reality television shows, training programs and books about how to make money and get-rich-quick investing in real estate, one would think that it would be relatively easy. The reality is that to succeed takes a lot of knowledge, particularly local knowledge, and the right mindset. We frequently meet with new investors whose money is "burning a hole in their pocket". They want to make an offer the instant they find something that looks good on paper. Our first step with a new investor is to educate on what they did not learn when they read or watched how to make money in real estate. As much as we want to make a sale every day, it's more important to make sure our clients make the very best choices whether they are investing, or purchasing or selling their own home.

What Clients Are Saying:

"Having worked with Leslie Dale for the past several years, I would highly recommend her to others looking to buy, sell

or manage real estate in the Charlotte and Gastonia area. As a lifelong resident of the area, her market knowledge is irreplaceable! Her qualities truly are too numerous to list; however, professionalism and listening skills are at the top. Listening is a talent not all realtors possess. It saves everyone time, energy and most importantly money! She understands what we need to accomplish and helps us achieve success. Leslie has shown us hundreds of properties and manages dozens of properties for us. We rely upon her as an integral part of our real estate team. The bottom line is Leslie gets results and does so with great communication, follow through and professionalism!"

- Will W.

"Leslie Dale is a great real estate agent. She helped us extensively when it came to purchasing a home. We were looking for a rental property and Leslie assured us that we were in a position to buy a home and to stop burning our hard earned money on rent. That revelation led us to purchasing a much better home than we thought possible. Leslie gave us the confidence that we were lacking, and made the effort on our behalf to get us a great deal!

We are happy here at our new home thanks in large part to Leslie Dale. She has a warm welcoming style and approach to the real estate business that seems to be a rare quality in an agent. I would highly recommend her for all of your real estate needs!"

- Lsbrown74

"We are just thrilled with the service Linda provided as our real estate agent for the sale of our home in Mount Holly. From advice on improvements to get our house move-in ready, to referrals of exceptional contractors to help with upgrades, to marketing our house and getting it under contract in FIVE DAYS, we couldn't have asked for more!

Linda's team kept us informed all along the way as we moved from the contract to the closing table for a really swift and smooth transaction. We're so pleased that we know Linda and look forward to working with her again when we are ready to sell or investment property."

- Alan and Terri J.

"Linda was instrumental in helping us secure the home of our dreams. Her wealth of knowledge of real estate assisted us through the contract and closing of our property. We highly recommend her for your personal realtor."

- J. and J. M.

About Leslie J. Dale

Leslie J. Dale, a native of the Charlotte area, began her residential real estate career in 2005 after nearly twenty years in commercial real estate and property management. She is a licensed broker in both North Carolina and South Carolina. Leslie has an international client list of investors who appreciate her knowledge of the area, current trends, future development and expertise in evaluation of income properties. She also has a loyal list of local clients who have relied on her wisdom and knowledge in transaction after transaction.

Leslie received the RE/MAX Hall of Fame Award in 2014, recognizing her as a top producer during her career with RE/MAX. She has also annually earned the RE/MAX Top Producer 100% Club Award. Leslie has been named by Charlotte Magazine as a Five Star Real Estate Agent in Client Satisfaction for the past several years.

For more information about Leslie J. Dale, visit http://www.LeslieDale.RemaxAgent.com.

About Linda Beverley

Linda Beverley is a Realtor with RE/MAX Executive in Charlotte, NC. She is a licensed broker in North Carolina and South Carolina. She began her career as a Realtor in 2003 after twenty years in management in the food industry. In addition to helping buyers and sellers with their home transactions, she assists local and long distance investors to find properties that work for their short-term and long-term investment portfolios. She also helps her investors by overseeing rehab projects on short-term investments as well as taking on a property management role for their long-term investments.

Linda has received the RE/MAX Executive Realty Top Producer 100% Club Award for several years and has also been named by Charlotte Magazine as a Five Star Real Estate Agent in Client Satisfaction for several years. She has received certifications from GRI (Graduate of Realtor Institute), E-Pro (social media technology) and CNE (certified negotiation expert).

For more information about Linda Beverley, visit http://www.LindaBeverley.com.

Chapter 10

Kim and Dick York

Greater Northeast Charlotte Real Estate

Real estate has been our passion for years; having bought and sold numerous personal properties, served as the general contractor for three of our homes, and moved several times, including long distance moves from Maine and Virginia. During that time, we have lived in different styles of properties – from a log house in the country to lake front property and have rented as well. Since moving to the greater Charlotte area in 1996 and enjoying the area lifestyle so much, we decided to focus on our passion by becoming North Carolina real estate brokers and assisting others with their real estate needs. All of our personal real estate experiences, coupled with extensive course work and knowledge, have been invaluable in working with both buyers and sellers interested in all different types of properties from condos, townhouses, and single-family homes, to short sales, golf course and lake front properties, active adult communities, and raw land. We have marketed and sold across the full spectrum of prices – from $50,000 lots to $3,500,000 estates - and geography - from south Charlotte to the I-40 corridor in the north and from Cabarrus and Rowan Counties in the east to Lincoln and Gaston Counties in the west – wherever referrals and our clients take us. Typically, our focus is the Greater Northeast of Charlotte, which has many Fortune 500 companies. With a great business environment, the Charlotte metro area has been among the fastest growing in the United States and is attracting many large business relocations and transfers. As members of multiple relocation teams, we help numerous transferees coming from around the country and the world. The Charlotte area has seen significant real estate investment activity as well. We have also helped local, out-of-area, and international investors to identify and purchase profitable investment properties.

Dick has a background in the forest industry, where he was purchasing large tracts of land and he has continued to represent sellers in large acreage raw land sales to developers and municipal parks and recreation departments. He also has been involved with the home construction process, which has proved to be a valuable asset to our clients. Kim was an educator and school administrator and she has always enjoyed helping people and educating them through the entire buying/selling process; she is also a certified home stager. We are certified specialists in negotiations, e-marketing, new home construction and relocation. Together we provide a unique blend of talents that work very well to achieve successful results for our real estate clients.

Selling Your Greater Northeast Charlotte Property

When a homeowner wants to sell their property, they primarily are interested in knowing how to price the property, what needs to be done to get the property ready for showings, and how long it will take to sell. Our two-step approach begins by doing initial research on the property, the neighborhood and recent comparable sales, using data from the local tax service and the Multiple Listing Service (MLS). At our first meeting with the homeowners, this information is shared along with highlights of the market conditions. Another part of our first meeting is dedicated to a discussion of the sales process, any timing constraints, finances associated with the sale, plans for their next home, and other questions/concerns they may have as all of this should be taken into consideration when selling a property.

During the initial visit, we will walk throughout the house, room-by-room, making a comprehensive listing of all of the details and discussing the features and upgrades that buyers are generally looking for in their next home. As part of the walk-through, we identify opportunities where minor upgrades can be made that could enhance the salability and pricing of the property, offer staging suggestions and also educate on what appraisers will be looking for when they come to appraise the property for buyer financing. A tour of the lot, garage and any outbuildings gives us a complete understanding of what the property offers.

A final pricing analysis is then completed which includes average days on the market, list-to-sale price ratio, and determination of the comparable sales in the area over the past 6 months. During the second visit, we share recommendations on a pricing range that is supported by the data. After educating the sellers on their property and the marketplace, they make an informed decision on the listing price of their property based on the facts. If the seller is seeking the highest price, it may take a little longer to generate the buyer, but if the seller is motivated to sell rapidly and has a commitment to a house or job on the other end, perhaps, then they need to be a little more aggressive with the pricing to generate a buyer quickly.

Buyers are doing most of their preliminary research online so it is critical that the property have great Internet exposure and that the online photography expresses a positive feel for the property. For a typical house, at least fifty to sixty interior and exterior photographs with different angles, views and elevations will be used in the marketing. As part of the staging process, we work with the seller to remove the distractions from areas being photographed. Certain colors or unique objects in a photo might draw the buyer's eye to that object, rather looking at the entire room. We also have a photo library of amenities in and surrounding the neighborhood that are included in our online marketing. These photos might include shops, schools, parks and recreational opportunities that are available in close proximity to the property.

Currently, our properties are marketed on 725 web sites. Typically the photos seen online are coming from the MLS and there will be anywhere from 4 to 24 photos posted. To ensure our properties are seen, we enhance the online posting to include at least 50 photos, as buyers love to see pictures, and we provide additional written descriptions. As our sellers know, buyers that tour their house are serious as they have seen many photos and know they like the house before even stepping inside. When searching online, buyers may see thousands of homes in the search results, and if a listing is not showing up in the top twenty-five or fifty homes, few buyers will likely see the online listing. We also currently offer premium placement packages on 8 well-known web sites. This, coupled with the fact that so many photos are posted, ensures our listings will show up near the top and will be seen by buyers.

In 15-20 seconds a buyer determines whether they like the property by the photos seen online. Since Kim is a home stager, as well as a broker, she will make recommendations to the homeowners about items that will enhance the showings of the home, such as moving furniture to give the room a more open feel or removing rugs that are covering up nice hardwood or tile floors. Sometimes, excess and/or personal items need to be put in storage, as buyers need to visualize themselves and their personal items in the house. We really want to provide our knowledge and expertise to the sellers so the property will be attractive to the majority of buyers. If a seller's goal is to sell in the shortest amount of time and at the highest price as possible, you really want to work with an agent that is upfront and honest with you about what the market is looking for, what buyers may take exception to, and how important the appearance of the property is for showings. Proper attention needs to be given to the outside of the property as well, because curb appeal will help attract a buyer. We actually have seen situations where potential buyers decided to not even get out of the car because the curb appeal was missing.

Some homeowners have misconceptions on the return on investments made for improvements. Many have invested large sums to improve their properties over a few years and expect that the investment will be returned when they sell the property. There are a number of television shows about home improvement and frequently the message that homeowners seem to hear is that making improvements to your property will increase the value. The reality is that some of the best improvements, like kitchen or bath renovations, generally only return about 60% of the investment. Many other improvements will return less than 50% of the cost. When our homeowners ask us about making improvements, we advise them to make the improvements for their enjoyment and to realize that those improvements may cause a buyer make an offer on their property over another one, but that the marketplace value may not pay for the full amount of the improvement. Backyard hardscapes with fireplaces and outdoor kitchens is a prime example for homeowners to enjoy all the wonderful benefits of these upgrades while living there and recognize that the next homeowner will be drawn to the property because of this improvement, but may not want to pay for entire cost of the upgrade.

There are several factors that sellers should consider when selecting an agent and a real estate company to market their property. They should choose an agent that makes real estate their full time business and has had many real estate experiences so as to be a great advisor. This agent will need to perform research, be able to recommend a proper market price range for the property, be able to advise on how to get a property ready to market, must have knowledge about the marketplace and buyers, and be able to negotiate contracts. Sellers should also consider the marketing plan that the agent will use to expose the property to the largest amount of relevant prospective buyers and to real estate agents. As mentioned earlier, Internet exposure today is critical, so sellers should expect that the agent will describe a plan that helps position the property at the top of searches for the price point. Also make sure that your agent has a professional approach to the photos to showcase your property in the best possible light. Since buyers from all over the nation and world are looking for their next home, choose a real estate company that has national exposure and experience. National ads, TV and Internet exposure is the key to being seen by buyers. Real estate companies that have relocation teams and departments to assist companies in making corporate moves is also an important factor in determining who should market your property.

Having won sales awards is an indicator of an agent that is successful in closing sales. It is also a good idea to check testimonials and reviews of past clients. Sellers will be working with the agent for a critical objective, so they will want to select an agent where there is a personal compatibility and good temperament and also one they feel they can trust to get the property sale successfully closed.

What Sellers Are Saying:

"Kim and Dick York offered superb service from start to finish. We worked with them almost a year before we put the house on the market; they pointed out several steps we could take to help the house and yard show better. They set us up with a great handyman, a flooring service, and a landscaping contractor, and followed up in every case to make sure we received quality service. When time came to list the house, Kim and Dick staged the rooms for great photos, identified the strengths of the property, maximized publicity on various media platforms, and remained available at a moment's notice for questions. The result: listed on a Friday afternoon, 20 showings in 3 days, and by Monday three offers, including one above asking price with no closing costs! Even when a minor snafu arose at the closing, Kim and Dick stepped in to offer a workable solution. We have the highest regard for their expertise."

- Kathie T. and Raymond S.

"I was very happy to meet Kim and Dick York. They were extremely professional. Being prior military, my wife and I have bought and sold many houses though the years. We chose Kim and Dick because we felt their knowledge of the market and years of experience set them apart from many other realtors. But that was only part of our decision making process. Since we were living out of state and the house we were selling was a rental we had to have someone with extensive contacts for repairs and very responsive over phone, e-mail and text.

Kim and Dick went above and beyond in getting repair estimates and following up, staging the house and providing me with honest feedback on issues as they arose. They were candid with us about the market and potential buyers. They even planted flowers in front of the door to make it look taken care of and homey to buyers. As a result we sold our house on the first day it was on the market.

It was great working with them. I would definitely recommend them to both buyers and sellers in the future."

- Scott & Tracy D.

Buying Your Greater Northeast Charlotte Property

Buyers are not only buying a home, they are buying a lifestyle. When starting to work with buyers, it is important that we, as agents, assist and understand their needs and preferences, such as number of bedrooms and bathrooms, size of home, type of property, price budget, nearby services and amenities and, of course, the location. Most local buyers have a good idea of the general location where they want to look for their next home. Out-of-town buyers typically know where they want to live based on what is bringing them to the Charlotte area and what they would like to have close by such as shopping, highway, golf courses, and schools. These people, who are moving into the area, will need guidance and often they will not have an idea of where the homes they have seen online are located.

After gathering the buyer's general property criteria and knowing the place of employment and/or reason for moving to a specific area, a review of what locations make sense, based on traffic patterns and the maximum length of commute desired is shared with the client. If given the opportunity, we first like to spend about a half-day touring around the Charlotte area, so buyers can get a feel for the high points and will be able to recognize locations when on their own. The tour would cover the Uptown/Center City area with the many sports, entertainment, cultural and dining amenities; the beautiful historic neighborhoods near Uptown; shopping malls; and a number of suburban neighborhoods. We will focus on a few neighborhoods that will provide a reasonable commute time. People unfamiliar with the area can get a pretty good feel for locations they will be comfortable with after experiencing the tour. Next, we will spend the remaining day and additional days looking at neighborhoods and properties that meet their criteria and that will work from a location standpoint.

Buyers are advised to work upfront with at least one lender to get pre-qualified for financing so they will know the price range they will be targeting. We suggest that buyers tell loan advisors what amount of money they feel most comfortable for having as a monthly payment. A buyer may qualify for a higher loan, but really want a different lifestyle that affords them the ability to do many other activities. In today's market, sellers will not consider an offer unless the buyer can show proof of pre-qualification or pre-approval of a loan, and most of the time, sellers do not even want their house shown unless the buyer is at least pre-qualified.

When finalizing a decision on a property, buyers should review any restrictions on the property that could possibly prevent use in the manner they intended, including any possible expansion they may desire in the future. Sometimes buyers want to add fences and pools, expand the deck, or build a screen porch. Reviewing any covenants and restrictions (CCRs) is very important to see what, if any, rules there are in the neighborhood. A consideration with most rural properties, and even in some neighborhoods, is that many are served with private or community wells and have septic tanks on the property. The homeowner will be responsible for any maintenance and replacement, if necessary, and building over the septic field will not be possible.

When a buyer decides that a property is a good match for their next home, they will want advice on the market value before making an offer. Research is done and a list is compiled of recent sales of similar properties in the neighborhood and/or nearby areas to provide a good basis for the value and to structure the offer. We discuss all the aspects of the contract, determine appropriate dates, and review buyer responsibilities per the contract.

After the purchase contract is negotiated and accepted, the buyer has a period of time, spelled out in the agreement, to complete their due diligence on the property. This is the time to complete all of the structural and mechanical inspections including a termite inspection, to request a survey, to have the house appraised, to get the loan approved, and to ask any other questions about the property, neighborhood and area. We will provide a list of recommended service providers for these tasks and will help with interpretation of the reports, as well. A survey is always recommended to make sure the buyer knows exactly the property limits and to make sure fences and buildings are not encroaching from either side of the boundary. If the property is served with a private well and/or septic system, an inspection on those systems and a water quality test is highly recommended. Sometimes a radon test is conducted, especially in areas where there can be a risk. Once the inspections are complete, we assist the buyer in developing a list of items to be addressed by the seller.

When selecting a real estate agent, buyers need to determine the agent's knowledge of the entire home buying process, from listening to what features you want in your next home to what you need to bring to the closing table. The agent should be able to discuss the positives and negatives of a property with you, prepare a market analysis, give advice on negotiating the contract, be actively involved in the inspection and repair process, be able to review the closing statement, and be available to you after the sale. Relocating buyers will want to work with agents that are certified relocation specialists. These specialists are knowledgeable about the entire relocation process, and that will be familiar with many communities the buyer can be shown with neighborhoods most suitable for them. They will want to work with an agent that has the patience to show them a full range of areas and neighborhoods to consider and one that they can enjoy working with and feel has a good personal chemistry. Buyers are also encouraged to check agent reviews and testimonials from past clients. Working with an agent that is a sales leader and has many years of experience in the area will increase the chances of a successful home purchase.

What Buyers Are Saying:

"Dick and Kim York are true professionals in the real estate industry. Buying a house can be stressful, they were a great team providing us with the help we needed in narrowing down our search and providing both emotional support and always looking out for our best interest when it came down to cost, the condition of the home and figuring out the best fit for our lifestyle. They were always quick to respond to any request or question that we had. We ended up buying in a great area!

Thanks again Kim and Dick!"

- Laurie and Eric L.

*"We met Kim York on one of the coldest days of winter in
Huntersville. We had just moved to the Charlotte area from
sunny southern California. Wow, what a change that was.
I'm not sure my husband and I were really prepared, but
Kim assured us that she and Dick would help us find a home
that would fit our needs. We needed to purchase with our
price range, be close to work, and have a floor plan that
was manageable, meaning not too big and not too
small. Our first day we viewed one home, drove around the
area with Kim as our expert guide, and then we met Dick at
Panera Bread to place an offer on the home we toured. Our
offer was not accepted, and I'm so thankful. One more day
with Kim and viewing three homes, and bang, we found the
one! She helped us so much with our choice by asking
questions that grounded our decision. The next few days,
Dick brought papers for signing to our extended stay, and
also took my husband on a tour of Charlotte. Our home
buying process with Dick and Kim was detailed, personal,
and efficient because of their many years of real estate
experience. Dick made sure the home inspection was
properly conducted and the necessary repairs were made
before we moved. So please, do yourself a big favor when
buying your next home in the Charlotte area, and get
together with Dick and Kim York!"*

- James and Jana C.

Featured Greater Northeast Charlotte Neighborhoods and Areas

Living in Charlotte's Greater Northeast area offers a fantastic lifestyle and a wide range of benefits. Just 10 miles out of Uptown, Charlotte's center city, you will have easy access to the major highways – I-85, I-77, I-485 and the new light rail system – taking you in all different directions. The Northeast offers beautiful parks, close proximity to three lakes – Lake Norman, Mountain Island Lake, High Rock Lake – numerous golf courses, convenient medical facilities, great schools, and all the benefits of living by a major campus, the University of North Carolina at Charlotte. There is lots of shopping – Concord Mills and NorthLake Malls, IKEA, Trader Joes - and entertainment, including the outdoor amphitheater, Charlotte Motor Speedway, sports complexes and so much more. Living between the ocean and the mountains is wonderful too; you can be on the Blue Ridge Parkway in an hour and a half and the beach in about 4 hours. Because the land is plentiful north of Charlotte, the properties are more affordable. We have lived north of Charlotte for years and absolutely love all that it offers.

From neighborhoods offering resort style amenities including pools and water parks, golf courses and tennis courts to rural communities, with larger lots and no HOA fees, the Greater Northeast Charlotte has so many different types of neighborhoods that buyers have a plethora to choose from when searching for their next home and lifestyle. Listed below is just a sampling of neighborhoods – from new construction to established feel – giving you an idea for what is offered in the Greater Northeast.

Abbington

Abbington is an upscale neighborhood offering a diverse range of properties from quality-built single family houses starting at $300,000 to luxury, custom built houses selling up to $900,000. Located in sought-after Harrisburg in Cabarrus County, it is minutes from Harrisburg Village,

Rocky River Road, I-485, I-85, UNCC, and Concord Mills Mall. This wooded neighborhood has a relaxed and leisurely feel and offers a pool, playground, and clubhouse. Along with great schools, all of the above make this a very desirable location and neighborhood.

Baileys Glen

Nestled between a community park, schools, and 2 major highways is an active adult community called Baileys Glen. The neighborhood offers a majority single family ranch plans and about 100 condos ranging in size from around 1300 – 3500 square feet and in the $250,000-$500,000 price point. The focal point of the neighborhood is the fantastic clubhouse with full-time activities director, game room, pool, and much more. Join in on the scheduled trips and community functions or enjoy relaxing on your screen porch or rocking chair front porch. This neighborhood is located in Cornelius, Mecklenburg County.

Christenbury

Christenbury has seven villages (Hall, Chase, Glen, Mews, Wood, Trace, Walk) offering different features from the gated, luxury homes village ranging from $700,000 to $1,300,000, to the mid-priced single family villages of $300,000-$600,000, and the townhouse village in the $250,000-$350,000 range. The stunning clubhouse and pool area, together with the all inclusive amenity package including fitness center, playground, walking trails, tennis courts, and rec area makes this a sought-after neighborhood. Christenbury is about 5 minutes to restaurants, shops, mall, I-85, I-485, and quality schools. In about 15 minutes you are in Uptown, at the gourmet restaurants, cultural and major sporting events and much more. Residents appreciate the ease of getting everywhere easily.

Davis Lake

Close to NorthLake Mall, UNCC, I-77, I-85; Davis Lake is a planned neighborhood of about 800 homes including condos and patio houses. Amenities include a pool, water park, tennis courts, volleyball court, 14-acre fishing lake, playground, 2 miles of walking and biking trails, and a soccer field. Residents enjoy a Farmer's Market, summer camps, and numerous planned community events. A short walk or bike ride finds you at restaurants and shops. This established neighborhood is minutes to Charlotte-Douglas Airport, Uptown, Lake Norman, golf courses and parks. Condos start at $100,000 to custom built houses around the lake that are $300,000 and higher.

Highland Creek
Highland Creek is Charlotte's north side Crown Jewel, offering a 3-mile gorgeous parkway lined with trees. Located between I-77 & I-85 and just north of the I-485 beltway, it has been the best selling neighborhood for years. Situated in Mecklenburg and Cabarrus Counties, the affordable housing ranges from $200,000 - $500,000 with single family, patio houses, and houses on the golf course. The amenities include an 18 hole public golf course, pools, water park, tennis courts, miles of walking trails, fitness center, planned community events and security patrol. Elementary and middle schools are located just off Highland Creek Parkway and other schools are minutes away. There is a day-care, nursing home, and memory impaired facility in Highland Creek. Concord Mills and NorthLake Malls, Trader Joes, IKEA are nearby, along with many restaurants.

Laurel Park
Laurel Park is about 25 minutes north of Uptown and just off I-85 in Concord, Cabarrus County. From craftsman styled to customized houses in the price range of $250,000 - $600,000, the neighborhood has a friendly feel with the tree lined sidewalks, a park and a pond. Amenities include a pool, tennis courts, playground, clubhouse, rec area and planned community events. Residents enjoy relaxing and dining at Afton Village and then go across the interstate to all the shopping you would need including Target, Stein Mart and Best Buy. Concord Mills is just down the interstate.

Old Stone Crossing

Old Stone Crossing offers a fun-filled lifestyle including pools, playgrounds, tennis courts, and clubhouses. Located just inside I-485 and off Back Creek Church Road in Mecklenburg County, you are just minutes from Concord Mills Mall, UNCC, medical facilities, and I-85. Uptown is about 10 miles away. The neighborhood offers townhouses and single family houses in the price range of $100,000 to customized houses in the $400,000s. Surrounded by a 40-acre nature preserve, along with 40 acres of woodlands in the neighborhood, this community has a peaceful county feel.

Skybrook

Rolling hills and resort style living are part of what draws homeowners to Skybrook, another public 18 hole golf course community. Home prices range from $250,000-$750,000 with many styles of houses from all brick siding to quaint cottage style. There are golf course lots, single family houses and townhouses. Skybrook offers pools, tennis courts, sports fields, playgrounds, ponds, and club complex. The amenities are offered as a smorgasbord – join the ones that you want to enjoy. Skybrook is between I-85, I-77, and north of I-485; is located in Cabarrus and Mecklenburg Counties; is minutes to shopping, restaurants, and lakes; and has expanded to include Skybrook North and Parkside.

The Villages of Leacroft

Looking for that wonderful established and quaint feeling neighborhood including mature landscaping and large lots? You have found Home in The Villages of Leacroft, which is in Mecklenburg County and offers tennis courts, a pool, playground and planned community events. Residents love the fact that they can walk/bike to shops and restaurants and the schools are minutes away. Situated between I-77 and I-85, NorthLake and Concord Mills Malls, and just south of I-485; you will have fantastic access in every direction. Within 5 minutes there are numerous Fortune 500 Companies and a Research Park. Houses in The Villages of Leacroft are selling in the $150,000 - $300,000 price range.

Winding Walk

An all Shea-built neighborhood, Winding Walk is located in Cabarrus County. Amenities include a beautiful clubhouse, pools, tennis courts, playground and walking trails. Construction started in the early 2000s and was completed in 2015 with the price ranges from $250,000 - $650,000. This community has a relaxing, rural feel yet is minutes to I-85, I-77 & I-485. Concord Mills Mall and great local schools are about 5 minutes away. There are three golf courses within 10 minutes and Lake Norman is about a 15-minute drive. Homeowners enjoy meeting at several nearby restaurants and the convenience of grocery and drug stores.

About Kim and Dick York

Kim and Dick York moved to Charlotte in 1995 after previously living in the Northeast and Virginia and started working in real estate in 1996. They are associated with Coldwell Banker United, Realtors in the Greater Northeast Charlotte office and are licensed in North Carolina.

Dick is a graduate Forester and worked in forestry, building products and new home construction prior to his becoming a Realtor. Kim has a B.S. Degree in Human Development/Education and a Masters Degree in Administration. She worked as an Educator and Administrator at the pre-school through college level before becoming a Realtor.

Kim and Dick York have won a number of awards of distinction. They were recognized as the #1 Coldwell Banker United, Realtors Agent in the Greater Charlotte area in 2014 and also were recognized as a member of the International Presidents Circle. Coldwell Banker Realtors lists them in the Top 4% of all agents worldwide. Charlotte Magazine has voted them as a Five Star Real Estate Agent in Client

Satisfaction annually since 2008. They were also one of only eleven agents in the greater Charlotte area to be recognized by Realtor.com for the Online Marketing Award of Excellence. The Yorks are members of three Coldwell Banker United, Realtors relocation teams that have received Platinum Awards for Excellence.

Kim and Dick also have a number of industry certifications including Certified Relocation Specialist, Certified EMarketing Specialist, Certified Negotiations Specialist, Certified Stager and Certified New Home Specialist.

For more information about Kim and Dick York, visit:
http://www.CBUnited.com/TheYorks
http://www.faceboook.com/KimandDickYork

Contact them at:
Homes@KimandDickYork.com
704-607-1256

Chapter 11

Brenda Thompson

Unique Mountain Properties

I've never fit "the mold", so why create a real estate firm that fits a mold! The idea of Special "Finds..." developed from my personal experiences as a buyer and seller before I became a real estate agent.

As a buyer, I wanted to own something different. I wanted to live in something unusual. *I wanted a property where my unique personality would feel at home.* Getting that point across to a typical agent was challenging. My agents are trained to help buyers recognize what type property will fit best with their unique personalities!

As a seller, when it came time to sell one of my unusual properties, I knew I had to make the most of its uniqueness. Since I come from a long line of writers and poets, I decided to use poetry to describe my listings.

In 1995 my company was born. The concept is a true extension of my unusual personality. As former director of marketing for the New York Stock Exchange, I've combined my love for unusual properties, my marketing expertise, and my poetry, to create my company. Special "Finds..."... Properties of Unique Character for Those Choosing Something Out of the Ordinary.

Our agency is focused on selling unique and unusual properties in the North Carolina Mountains. A Special "Find..." is sometimes hard to define, but it is certainly not the mass-produced houses seen in the typical subdivision. Although many of our listings are luxury properties, a Special "Find..." doesn't have to be expensive. It might be rare or hard to find and sometimes is weird or funky. A Special

"Find..." can be unique because of its setting. It often has an unusual interior floor plan. Historic or antique houses are always Special "Finds..." as they're not making any more of them.

Our office is located in Asheville. We help homeowners sell their unique properties across the western North Carolina Mountains within about two to three hours of Asheville. Our buyers literally come from around the globe.

Selling Your Unique Mountain Property

If you own a unique house, consider yourself lucky! You have something to advertise that other properties may not have. Use your property's uniqueness to make it stand out from the crowd. When selling an unusual property, recognize that there is a value in having something that is one-of-a-kind. Make sure to feature all of the special characteristics in marketing the property and don't waste time and money in trying to market to ordinary buyers who aren't looking for something unique or unusual. I would encourage sellers to make sure their agent has a plan on how they will market to buyers who are seeking a unique property.

One of the first things sellers of unique properties want to know is: "How do I price my home?" Pricing unusual properties is not quite the same as pricing a property in a traditional neighborhood or subdivision where comparable sales can be found in close proximity. To find enough comparable sales to properly price a property, we often have to extend our search area quite a distance. With our focus on unusual properties, we catalog all unique listings in our market area, and provide that as a resource for buyers through our SpecialFinds.com website. We monitor unique properties as they sell, and have a database of unique property sales we can use for pricing analyses. Sellers are advised to make sure their agent can demonstrate a professional approach to pricing the property, taking into consideration the unique characteristics, and the challenge in finding comparable sales.

A common mistake that sellers make is to insist on an unrealistically high listing price, believing that they are creating room for negotiations and that they can reduce the price later if the listing is not attracting buyers. Although it is difficult to properly establish a market price for a unique property, buyers are more educated than in the past and most of the time can sense that a property is priced well above a fair price. The most common result is a small amount of showings or no showings, no offers, and therefore, no negotiations. The recommended approach is to price the property in a realistic range, attracting the highest number of interested buyers.

There are buyers specifically looking for unusual properties, and sellers want to make sure they are attracting these buyers for their unique property. Buyers of unique properties buy on emotions, so they first need to emotionally connect with the property and then they will consider the facts. Sellers of these properties will want to work with an agent that can verbalize the unique characteristics of the property so potential buyers will relate to it.

We use stories in our listings to bring the properties to life, so that a buyer can "mentally" feel what it will be like to live there, and to be on the property. I like to bring as many senses as I can into the ads – what you see – floors the color of honey; what you hear – a train whistle in the distance; what you feel – cool slate floors; what you smell – fresh mown grass. I want to describe the property so the buyer can feel the history of the place. The marketing should mentally transport buyers to the property from wherever they are as they read the story. We try to give them a feeling of what it's like when the house in the description becomes their home.

Below are two examples of stories I have used in ads for unique home listings.

"Apogee"

As if reaching for the very stars above, music filled the space. "Turn it all the way up, no one can hear us!" And they did...and they danced. Friends called, and 17 minutes later they met them downtown for dinner. Apogee, at a cooler 3950', is the highest altitude Asheville address. Totally private with 75 mile views, she sits on 14.6, low maintenance, mostly wooded acres, sharing a .25 mile boundary with the Blue Ridge Parkway. With 6420 sq. ft., there are views from every room. Numerous porches & decks invite entertaining or reflection. A few of the high-end features include: 2 master suites, ultra-luxurious ensuite bath, Crow's Nest for star gazing; 2-story, stacked-stone, wood burning fireplace, enormous kitchen, both formal and relaxed spaces, hardwood & radiant heat tiled floors, wired sound system and closets aligned to incorporate an elevator. Awe-inspiring Asheville city lights.

"The Old Allison Place – 70 Acres"

Every Sunday, sinners and saints showed up at Grandma Allison's house. No invitation necessary, no shortage of food – fried chicken, mashed potatoes and gravy, fried okra, and more. The kitchen was crowded, yet we all fit in -- buttermilk biscuits hot out of the oven. Prayer, then pass the dishes – all gone. Kids everywhere, slamming doors, hiding in the bedrooms upstairs and down. Out in the big barn, men discuss livestock, and when or if to cut the timber again. Women relax on the wraparound porch. Banana pudding for dessert! Sitting on 70+ acres, with approximately 55 in woods.

Buyers often inquire about our listings by name or by elements of the house's story, rather than the address. They will ask about "the house where the seven children grew up", or "the place where the horses waited for the sound of the sliding barn door". An interesting result of our descriptive advertising is that we have sold four of our listings to remote buyers just from the advertising without the buyer ever physically seeing the properties until coming to the closing table. We use detailed photography and video tours, so in any case the buyer did have a virtual tour. We had the buyers agree to hold the sellers and our firm harmless if they didn't like the property once they saw it, and each one closed without an issue.

Regardless the type of property, it is always important that the house shows well, both on the outside as well as the interior. Make sure that the property is in very good condition and make sure that you keep it that way during the listing period. Be willing to show the property at any time. With an unusual property, make sure you are prepared to move when you have a buyer. When a buyer comes along there may not be ten of them looking for your property; there may only be one.

What sellers are saying:

"An interview with several real estate agents prompted me to list with Brenda. However, she did so much more than 'list.' She met with us to lay the foundation for how she would present this house. She then spent time on the property to enable her to write a story of the home that would convey its unique character to buyers. The buyer approached her so she functioned professionally as a dual agent. Brenda and her assistant helped both the buyer and seller to move through the process and were an excellent liaison during due diligence and on through closing...... which occurred within 2 months of our initial meeting!"

- Pat T.

"My knowledge of Brenda is based not only on her skills but more importantly on her attitude. She listens to what I have to say, then responds accordingly. I don't always like what I hear but I know that her facts are accurate. Brenda has a good heart. She understands how attached one can become

toward property and home and she treats that attachment with respect. Anyone can list a property but not all are willing to do the extra things needed to show and sell. Do yourself a favor. Start with the best. Brenda can be counted on to work hard to get the job done."

- Trudee S.

Buying Your Unique Mountain Property

The mountains of western North Carolina are an easy two-hour drive from Charlotte. Many Charlotte residents already have a vacation or retirement home here. Heading toward cooler temperatures and escaping the asphalt jungle on weekends is a common practice for Charlotte area residents. The WNC mountains offer almost every type lifestyle imaginable from championship golf courses, ski and lake resorts, city living in Asheville, to small eclectic communities nearby, or to get out into the country in just 20 minutes. You can hike the Appalachian Trail, paddle any number of rivers, or drive the Blue Ridge Parkway, just to name a few of the many outdoor activities. If people-watching is your thing, there's no better place to be than downtown Asheville! Housing choices range from adorable tiny houses, remote log cabins, organic farms, riverfront retreats, to expensive luxury estates. All price ranges are represented.

Since the mountain area is so large and the options so many, potential buyers from outside the area will want to narrow things down a bit before beginning their search for the perfect property. Two of the most important considerations are the budget and the type of area where you want to live. As an example, do you want to live close to conveniences such as shopping, restaurants and medical centers, or is your passion to be in proximity to recreation activities such as hiking, horseback riding trails, boating or skiing? These are not always mutually exclusive as we do have many communities that have both the modern conveniences as

150

well as recreational amenities in close proximity. You will also want to decide on the size of house you want including the number of bedrooms and bathrooms needed.

Is there is specific type of community where you would like to live? We have a large variety in the mountain area with communities focused on some recreational activities such as skiing, golf, equestrian and fishing and boating at rivers and lakes. There are communities focused on the arts and spiritual or holistic living. We have historic districts and gated-luxury communities. Another consideration is the amount of land you desire. Consider if you want to live in a city or town with close proximity to neighbors, or in a more isolated, rural setting.

These are just examples of some of the initial points buyers will want to consider before starting the search for a property. Once you have a pretty good idea of what you are looking for, it's time to contact an agent or start searching online. In addition to all of our own Special "Finds..." listings, we have put together a catalog of all listed unique properties in the mountain area, in one place, on our website. We review every property listing in the mountains and identify the ones we would classify as unique. We then sort them by style and type and organize them for buyers to review on SpecialFinds.com. These properties are sorted into the following categories: Log and Rustic Properties, Historic Properties, Water Front or Water View Properties, Horse Properties and Farms, Modern Green Eclectic Houses and Luxury Homes and Estates. SpecialFinds.com is the only place buyers can find virtually every listed unique property in the mountain area without having to wade through the clutter of ordinary properties seen on other real estate websites. We can tell by our web traffic that buyers will visit the site, often lingering for hours, searching thorough the various unique property listings.

What Buyers Are Saying:

"Brenda Thompson did a terrific job on helping us acquire he house on Church Hill Drive. She was able to answer all our questions and made many helpful suggestions on the buy process. She has a very good knowledge of what all the requirements are and has the ability to find the right people to help get the job done right. Brenda works hard to see that all your needs are fulfilled and she'll take care of even the smallest details. Home buying is a large investment and Brenda made the process as easy as possible. I highly recommend as a real estate agent."

- John T.

"It was a pleasure working with Brenda Thompson as our agent in buying our new home! She was always prompt in answering our calls and emails, was totally available, and knows her stuff! She went above and beyond the call of duty in terms of resource information that we asked for. While quite professional, she also was wonderful to relate to with a personable style."

- Jeanie C.

About Brenda Thompson

Brenda Thompson founded her Asheville-based, niche real estate company, Special "Finds...", in 1995. With the slogan "Properties of Unique Character for Those Choosing Something Out of the Ordinary", her company's sole focus is on selling unique and unusual properties. Brenda's unique brand of marketing integrates her poetic writings to "bring her listings to life". She was one of sixteen Finalists in the prestigious Make Mine a $Million Business® program sponsored by Count Me In for Women's Economic Independence, and founding partner, OPEN from American Express®. She is licensed in North Carolina, Pennsylvania and Maryland, and formerly licensed in New York.

For more information about Brenda and Special "Finds..." visit: http://specialfinds.com.

Chapter 12

Mike Waite

Selecting a Remodeling Contractor

I joined NARI as the Executive Director of the Greater
Charlotte Chapter in early 2012, after consulting for non-
profit organizations the prior ten years. NARI, The National
Association of the Remodeling Industry, is a not-for-profit
trade association that is the lone professional association
that is dedicated to the remodeling industry in the United
States. NARI encourages ethical conduct, sound business
practices and professionalism among its members and
educates, trains and offers programs for the region's most
respected remodelers.

My background includes delivering leadership training and
team building for a variety of non-profit organizations and
evolved into working with non-profits that were military-
related. I have also been one of the directors of the Business
Leaders of Charlotte since 2003. That organization is a good
partner with NARI in our philanthropic efforts in the region.

NARI's goal is to help consumers identify the right
professional partner for their remodeling projects and NARI
wants homeowners to get the maximum value and
enjoyment out of the money invested in their remodeling
projects. NARI's members are the professionals in
remodeling, the contractors that are not just passing
through. They don't just have a set of tools, a pickup truck
and a set of skills. They know how to run a business, they're
good citizens and they pay their bills. The members are really
the elite in the industry; they're the folks that are kind of
charged with carrying the flag for the remodeling industry.
Unfortunately the industry itself doesn't have such a great
reputation because there are a lot of unethical operators out
there that dupe homeowners. NARI members are the

professionals that seek out extra education and certifications and they want to set themselves apart from the other competitors in the industry.

The common thread of NARI is the code of ethics. All members agree to follow the code and conduct their business in an appropriate manner that all members are proud of. Even though new contractors may have years of skillful experience, they are not eligible to join NARI until their business has developed a track record and the business has been successfully operated for at least two years. NARI is a business membership, not an individual membership. Applicants for membership are vetted thoroughly and we verify licenses, insurance and status with the Secretary of State. NARI polices members once they are part of the organization as it is in the interest of all members to maintain the reputation that has been earned by participating in the association.

The core of the NARI membership are the design-build remodeling contractors, but there are many more contractor categories that are involved in home remodeling and NARI is the one place ethical companies involved in remodeling can come together to be a force for good business practices. Our membership includes everything from homebuilders that also handle remodeling projects to heating and air conditioning, electrical, plumbing, floor covering companies, landscaping, handyman services and many other categories. We have designers and architects and even manufacturers and suppliers. Supporting business service professionals like property, casualty and worker's comp insurance agents are also among our membership. We have the same code of ethics for all categories and the same vetting and background checks prior to joining.

Homeowners contemplating a remodeling project need to consider how involved they want to be in the process and their budget for the work. The most typical example is that homeowners choose to work with an interior design-build contractor that does everything in-house and you've got one point of contact. A design-build contractor has the full capabilities in house to make a design, get all of the permits and complete the renovation work. They more often than not sub out certain parts of the project to other contractors, but they manage the entire process.

Homeowners that want to be more involved might work initially with an interior designer to develop a written plan, but then they need to work with a contractor or a team of contractors to get the construction completed.

The remodeling contractor you select will be your partner for a period of time so it is important to work with one that you can trust and that you will be comfortable with being in your house for a period of time. You really want to select a contractor that operates like a solid business and not just someone who has trade skills. Check the contractor out with the local Better Business Bureau's website. Although a good record there doesn't rule out possible issues, most contractors that are not legitimate will have a poor record with the BBB. Most contractors have some complaints, but it is important to see how past consumer complaints have been handled and you can get a good sense of that on the BBB website. Most contractors will say they have a license, but ask for a copy of the license to make sure and if you have any doubts about the authenticity, check with the state licensing authorities.

Insurance is another critical point to check. Contractors need to have sufficient casualty and liability insurance coverage as well as worker's compensation insurance. Be sure to ask for a copy of the contractor's insurance certificates. If the contractor doesn't have liability insurance, the homeowner is at risk for damage to their property caused by the contractor. There is additional risk if the contractor caused damage to a neighbor's property. Lack of worker's compensation insurance puts the homeowner at risk if one of the contractor's personnel is injured on the job. Lack of proper insurance coverage is the sign of a less than legitimate contractor and many try to slide by without coverage.

Reference checks are another important part of a homeowner's due diligence. A lot of contractors provide client references, but very few people actually check the references. When checking references, find out how the contractor handled any warranty issues. Now it is possible that the contractor provides references that are from friends and those will all be good ones. A meaningful type of reference that homeowners rarely consider is to check with the contractor's suppliers. Suppliers can provide information about how they are paid and a poor record would be an important indicator of possible problems.

The general contractor usually subcontracts aspects of the work to other contractors, known a subcontractors, so it is also a good idea to inquire about the subcontractors that will be used and check references on them as well. If the general contractor checks out, hopefully they are working with well-qualified subcontractors that have proven themselves at a high level of professionalism, but they don't always know what the subcontractor reputations are.

Although it is normal for a contractor to require a deposit or some type of security to bind the work, a red flag is a contractor that requires a significant percentage of money upfront before work is started. Some dis-reputable remodelers are collecting money up front on one job to pay for the last job and that's not a solid business model. When they are undercapitalized, some contractors start cutting corners and not doing things in the right manner for the clients.

Inquire about the contractor's system for change orders, especially unplanned change orders. Reputable companies have good systems in place to communicate and document change orders. Some may say to just give a call and they can make it happen, but that's not a process. Again, you should work with contractors that operate like solid businesses.

There is a huge risk for homeowners if work is done without securing a building permit from the city or county. This is an area where many contractors cut corners to save money, being able to offer a lower price. The first risk is that the work may not be done in a safe manner, without inspections and not following local codes. This is also illegal. Remodeling is a big investment for the homeowner and when it comes time to sell the property, it is likely that improvements done without a permit will be discovered. The outcome in such cases is not good and most often involves fines and could even require that improvements be removed. Make sure your contractor gets all necessary permits and the work is inspected by the local building inspection agency.

Homeowners can also reduce their risk by considering and selecting NARI members to work with. They are the professionals of the remodeling industry, and in addition to having the right technical skill set, they've taken the extra time and the extra expense to get certifications and to do the continuing education. They uphold their licenses and they have appropriate insurance. They're better equipped for a long-term relationship and they have a history of longevity. Contractors would not be telling the truth if they said there never has been a problem with a job, because even the best have had some issues. The real difference is in how problems or warranty issues are handled and how professionals really shine in handling the problem, so it's not too much stress for the homeowner. You don't want a contractor that looks at a problem as something that is going to put them out of business. That's where a NARI contractor, that's had longevity, excels. They are rooted in running a good business instead of just selling things, and that's what really sets them apart.

Homeowners can find numerous resources on the local NARI Charlotte website at http://www.naricharlotte.com.

One very useful resource is the Membership Directory for Homeowners. The document provides background on NARI and the organization's Code Of Ethics, Purpose and Values. There is also a section that provides tips for homeowners looking to find a contractor to handle their project while minimizing risks.

The directory provides a listing of members, organized by the following categories:

- General Contractors Design/Build
- Appliance Suppliers
- Building Material Suppliers
- Business Services
- Carpentry and Painting
- Ceramic Tile, Marble, Granite & Natural Stone Suppliers & Installers
- Designers
- Education Services
- Electricians
- Floor Cover Contractors
- Handyman Services
- Heating and Air Conditioning Contractors
- Insulation Contractors/Manufacturers
- Kitchen and Bath Contractors
- Kitchen and Bath Suppliers
- Mold and Water Damage
- Painting Contractors/Manufacturers
- Plumbing Contractors
- Roofing and Siding Contractors
- Specialty Contractors
- Structural Specialists
- Waterproofing
- Windows, Doors, Siding & Sunroom Contractors

NARI members believe in giving back to the community and the organization conducts a number of fundraising activities throughout the year with proceeds going to worthy causes in the community.

About Mike Waite

Mike Waite is Executive Director for NARI of Greater Charlotte, the local chapter of the National Association of the Remodeling Industry. He is the Chair of NARI's Chapter Executive Forum, representing the Executive Directors from all 54 NARI markets on the NARI National Board of Directors, and facilitates the national Chapter Growth and Support Initiative across the country. Mike has lived in the Charlotte area since 1974, and has worked as a professional in the Charlotte-Metro market since 1985.

In addition to his multiple roles with NARI, Mike has been a director and board member of the Business Leaders of Charlotte (BLOC) since 2003, a Rotarian since 2004, a member of multiple chambers of commerce and the Cabarrus County Building Industries Association (CCBIA).

He has also been affiliated with the following non-profit organizations:
- Crime Victims Coalition – Board Member since 2008, President 2009/2010
- Leadership Cabarrus Alumnus (2009)/Steering Committee Member

- Charlotte Area Fund – Board of Directors (current)
  - Building Task Force, Fund-Raising Committee, and Job Readiness Instructor
- Computer Empowerment – Board of Directors and life skills instructor (2003 – 2008)
- Pro Bono Consultant – Wings of Eagles Ranch and Piedmont Residential Development Center

Mike is also a published author, having written a book on relationship based networking in the business-to-business market, titled "Networking Fuel: Who Needs to Know You?", which was published in February 2008.

For more information about NARI Charlotte, visit http://www.naricharlotte.com

www.ingramcontent.com/pod-product-compliance
Lightning Source LLC
Chambersburg PA
CBHW051916170526
45168CB00001B/408